S. HRG. 114–429

REGIONAL NUCLEAR DYNAMICS

HEARING

BEFORE THE

SUBCOMMITTEE ON STRATEGIC FORCES

OF THE

COMMITTEE ON ARMED SERVICES
UNITED STATES SENATE

ONE HUNDRED FOURTEENTH CONGRESS

FIRST SESSION

FEBRUARY 25, 2015

Printed for the use of the Committee on Armed Services

Available via the World Wide Web: http://www.fdsys.gov/

U.S. GOVERNMENT PUBLISHING OFFICE

22–491 PDF WASHINGTON : 2016

For sale by the Superintendent of Documents, U.S. Government Publishing Office
Internet: bookstore.gpo.gov Phone: toll free (866) 512–1800; DC area (202) 512–1800
Fax: (202) 512–2104 Mail: Stop IDCC, Washington, DC 20402–0001

COMMITTEE ON ARMED SERVICES

JOHN McCAIN, Arizona, *Chairman*

JAMES M. INHOFE, Oklahoma	JACK REED, Rhode Island
JEFF SESSIONS, Alabama	BILL NELSON, Florida
ROGER F. WICKER, Mississippi	CLAIRE McCASKILL, Missouri
KELLY AYOTTE, New Hampshire	JOE MANCHIN III, West Virginia
DEB FISCHER, Nebraska	JEANNE SHAHEEN, New Hampshire
TOM COTTON, Arkansas	KIRSTEN E. GILLIBRAND, New York
MIKE ROUNDS, South Dakota	RICHARD BLUMENTHAL, Connecticut
JONI ERNST, Iowa	JOE DONNELLY, Indiana
THOM TILLIS, North Carolina	MAZIE K. HIRONO, Hawaii
DAN SULLIVAN, Alaska	TIM KAINE, Virginia
MIKE LEE, Utah	ANGUS S. KING, JR., Maine
LINDSEY GRAHAM, South Carolina	MARTIN HEINRICH, New Mexico
TED CRUZ, Texas	

CHRISTIAN D. BROSE, *Staff Director*
ELIZABETH L. KING, *Minority Staff Director*

SUBCOMMITTEE ON STRATEGIC FORCES

JEFF SESSIONS, Alabama, *Chairman*

JAMES M. INHOFE, Oklahoma	JOE DONNELLY, Indiana
DEB FISCHER, Nebraska	BILL NELSON, Florida
MIKE LEE, Utah	JOE MANCHIN III, West Virginia
LINDSEY GRAHAM, South Carolina	ANGUS S. KING, JR., Maine
TED CRUZ, Texas	MARTIN HEINRICH, New Mexico

CONTENTS

FEBRUARY 25, 2015

REGIONAL NUCLEAR DYNAMICS

WEDNESDAY, FEBRUARY 25, 2015

U.S. SENATE,
SUBCOMMITTEE ON STRATEGIC FORCES,
COMMITTEE ON ARMED SERVICES,
Washington, DC.

The committee met, pursuant to notice, at 2:33 p.m. in room SR–220, Russell Senate Office Building, Senator Jeff Sessions (chairman of the subcommittee) presiding.

Committee members present: Senators Sessions, Fischer, Nelson, Donnelly, and King.

OPENING STATEMENT OF SENATOR JEFF SESSIONS, CHAIRMAN

Senator SESSIONS. Okay, the subcommittee would come to order, and I appreciate the good witnesses that we have. Senator Donnelly, thank you for your leadership and participation and dedication to helping us get this issue right.

I think we are close to having a bipartisan policy on this, which is not always possible in this body, but we have been able to operate pretty well as a subcommittee for quite a number of years, since I have been in the Senate now 18 years. Hard to believe.

Senator DONNELLY. I have almost been here that long.

Senator SESSIONS. It seems like it. So we had—our subcommittee on February 11th received a classified briefing on worldwide nuclear capabilities and threats, which revealed the scope and extent to which other nuclear powers are modernizing their weapon nuclear capabilities and increasing, it appears, reliance on nuclear weapons for their security.

Today's open hearing is meant to explore the implications of this global nuclear renaissance, renewal around the world, for U.S. nuclear strategy forces and declaratory policy. While the size and composition of the U.S. nuclear arsenal is driven primarily by the nuclear and conventional might of Russia and agreements with Russia, the expansion of nuclear arsenals across the globe, coupled with a growing regional tension, suggests that there are other factors that should inform U.S. nuclear policy and strategy.

We divided the world between four prominent think tank scholars. You each have the world in your hands. Dr. Andrew Krepinevich will look at the Middle East. Dr. Matthew Kroenig will focus on NATO [North Atlantic Treaty Organization]/Europe, while Dr. George Perkovich and Dr. Ashley Tellis will tackle Asia. They have been asked in general—we have asked you in general to look out about 10 years. Where are we, and where should we go?

A summary—and think about the following—a summary of the nuclear capabilities and doctrine of the nuclear and potential nuclear powers in their region, to include the rationale for acquiring nuclear weapons, the likelihood for a nuclear escalation, and implications for nuclear proliferation, which is a real—is reality, I am afraid.

Why is it important for the United States to manage nuclear stability in the regions, how difficult such a task might be? What might be the role of the United States during a regional crisis or conflict that could escalate to nuclear use? Finally, any recommendations for U.S. national security policy, nuclear force policy, and nuclear doctrine derived from your analysis.

On the President's budget request, I think it is fair to say affirms a policy of modernization. We will be looking to make sure that we are sufficiently funded for that. We are behind, some would suggest, at about $2.5 billion from what we agreed to when we started this bipartisan effort several years ago.

So this will be the order, as I understand it—Dr. Krepinevich, Dr. Kroenig, Dr. Tellis, and Dr. Perkovich. In that order we would go. All right.

Do you have any comments?

STATEMENT OF SENATOR JOE DONNELLY

Senator DONNELLY. Thank you, Mr. Chairman. I want to thank Chairman Donnelly and Senator Sessions for holding this hearing, which is to set the policy context for many of the issues that we face in the subcommittee this Congress. It follows on the footsteps of a highly successful hearing we had last year on how we deal with nuclear proliferation outside the United States-Russia context.

Let me also thank all of you for taking the time to testify here today. We very much appreciate your ideas, your thoughts, and your recommendations.

I want to concentrate first on the India-Pakistan nuclear question. This region seems to be an area where nuclear weapons are growing, with great potential for possible instability from a conventional conflict or from terrorism.

I also want to find out what these countries and their nuclear programs mean for the United States. We now know that India and China are developing ballistic submarines. What does this mean for the region and for the United States?

Finally, how can countries surrounding North Korea react to their nuclear program, and how can we help them?

Again, thank you for coming today. I look forward to the dialogue. Mr. Chairman, off we go.

Senator SESSIONS. Dr. Krepinevich?

STATEMENT OF ANDREW F. KREPINEVICH, JR., PRESIDENT, CENTER FOR STRATEGIC AND BUDGETARY ASSESSMENTS

Dr. KREPINEVICH. Thank you, Mr. Chairman, Senator Donnelly, for the opportunity to be here today and offer my views on these important issues. I will try and summarize my remarks in the form of four brief points.

First, of course, looking at the Middle East, which is my area. Right now, there is only one undeclared nuclear power in the region. However, obviously, there is the issue of Iran. While the negotiations to forestall Iran from becoming a nuclear power are in progress, from what is being reported in the press it seems likely that should an agreement along these lines be made, Iran will likely be a threshold nuclear power in 10 years. This perhaps is not surprising.

Given the current state of Iran's nuclear program, the immense cost Iran's leaders have invested in it, the great lengths to which they have gone to deceive the international community regarding their nuclear program, and the substantial advantages that would accrue to Teheran from possessing nuclear weapons, it seems unlikely that anything short of the threat or the use of force would deflect the current regime from its objective of achieving a nuclear weapons capability.

Second, while we can and should certainly hope for a positive breakthrough in the current negotiations, hope is not a strategy. Prudence dictates that we contemplate what challenges we might confront should these negotiations fail to arrest Iran's progress toward the bomb.

Should Iran acquire a nuclear capability, which is certainly plausible within the 5- to 10-year timeframe that you have asked us to examine, the initial bipolar nuclear competition between Iran and Israel, I would think, would be far less stable than the bipolar nuclear competition that existed between the United States and the Soviet Union during the Cold War for several reasons.

First, given the state of relations between Israel and Iran, there seems relatively little chance that the two sides will engage in mutual confidence-building measures, things such as hotlines or arms control or intrusive inspection regimes.

Second, the geography of the two countries means that missile flight times between the two would be far less than even 10 minutes, whereas during the Cold War we had arguably 20 to 30 minutes warning time of an attack by the Soviet Union.

Third, particularly with respect to Iran, early warning systems and command and control structures are likely to be limited at best, which may lead one or both sides to place their forces on hair-trigger alert or to extend nuclear weapons release authority down the chain of command, increasing the risk of unauthorized or accidental launch of a nuclear attack.

Fourth, the potential—with the rise of cyber warfare, the potential to covertly insert cyber weapons into command and control or early warning systems may further reduce the confidence either the Israelis or especially the Iranians might have in their ability to detect an attack. Again, all this may push both sides, particularly in a crisis, to a very hair-trigger kind of nuclear force posture, if you will, one that would certainly compromise efforts to reduce the risk of a nuclear use.

My third point is that a nuclear-armed Iran, or even an Iran that is a nuclear threshold state, could trigger a proliferation cascade in the region. If there is an Israeli bomb and a Persian Shia bomb, one could surmise that for their security, Arab states and perhaps the Turks as well would seek a nuclear capability.

Certainly in the open press, there are reports that, given the relationship that the Saudis have with the Pakistanis, Pakistan could, for example, deploy nuclear weapons on Saudi soil, somewhat similar to the way that we have nuclear weapons on Turkey's soil right now. Only the difference could be that the Saudis would have de facto control over those weapons. Or you could find an unraveling of the NPT regime, where the transfer of nuclear-related technology, the barriers to those transfers could become a lot lower.

In particular, even transfers of technology that do not relate directly to nuclear weapons themselves—such as the ability to miniaturize a nuclear warhead to fit on a ballistic missile, or the ability to develop cruise missiles and place them offshore, say, offshore of Israel or to provide even less warning time than Israel would have today, or of course precision guidance that would enhance the effectiveness of these weapons—could further destabilize an already unstable situation.

Fourth, should—I am sorry—should other states in the region besides Iran and Israel acquire nuclear weapons, of course, warning times could be reduced even further. Consider the example of Saudi Arabia and Iran. The two countries are very, very close together, obviously, and it seems difficult to imagine that you could have an effective early warning and command and control system to respond effectively to an attack.

So attack attribution may be difficult as well. In the sense that if early warning systems and command and control systems are limited, and there are four or five actors in the region and you are attacked, under certain circumstances it may be very difficult in the wake of an attack to accurately determine exactly who the perpetrator was.

My fourth point is that these could have significant effects on the U.S. military posture. One effect, certainly, would be an Iran that can operate behind a nuclear shield may be an even more aggressive sponsor of terrorism proxy war than it is today not only within the region, but perhaps beyond the region as well. Should we decide to pursue a strategy of extended deterrence, we may run into difficulties as well.

As you have pointed out, other states are modernizing their nuclear forces. China and Russia modernizing their forces as well, moving particularly the Russians toward smaller-yield weapons, weapons with focused effects. This provides them with more options in terms of how they might respond in a nuclear crisis. Right now, we are denying our President the ability to have that kind of flexibility in responding to a crisis.

Second, as one senior Arab statesman pointed out to me when we were discussing the issue of extended deterrence, "You Americans talk about extended deterrence. You extend deterrence to protect your allies against the Russians, the Chinese, the North Koreans, and now prospectively the Iranians. But you keep reducing your nuclear arsenal. So at the same time you are increasing your commitments, you are reducing your capabilities, and we find that a bit disturbing."

My final point is that Thomas Schelling once remarked that he felt it took U.S. strategists well over a decade following the introduction of nuclear weapons to arrive at a reasonably good understanding of the character of the United States-Soviet nuclear competition. This was achieved only after long and dedicated effort by talented strategists such as Bernard Brodie, Herman Kahn, Henry Kissinger, Andrew Marshall, and Albert and Roberta Wohlstetter, to name but a few.

While considerable effort by many talented analysts has been devoted to assessing how we might preclude Iran from acquiring nuclear weapons, given current trends, it seems prudent to hedge our bets and work to obtain as best we can a sense of what it means for our security to live in a world in which these efforts fail to prove out.

This completes my summary, Mr. Chairman. Thank you.

[The prepared statement of Dr. Krepinevich follows:]

CSBA

February 25, 2015

STATEMENT BEFORE THE SENATE ARMED SERVICES SUBCOMMITTEE ON STRATEGIC FORCES ON THE IMPLICATIONS FOR U.S. SECURITY OF GROWING NUCLEAR CAPABILITIES IN THE MIDDLE EAST

By Andrew F. Krepinevich
President
Center for Strategic and Budgetary Assessments

Mr. Chairman, Senator Donnelly, Members of the Committee, thank you for inviting me to appear before you today to present my thoughts on the implications of growing regional nuclear capabilities for U.S. security. As requested, I will focus my remarks on the situation in the Middle East over the next decade.[1]

U.S. SECURITY OBJECTIVES IN THE MIDDLE EAST

The United States arguably has three overriding security objectives in the Middle East. First, we have to eliminate sanctuaries for fanatical cults like ISIS from which they could mount catastrophic attacks against the U.S. homeland in the future. Second, we want to maintain access to the global economy's principal energy source. Third, we want to prevent the spread of nuclear weapons in the region, particularly to Iran, whose hostility to the United States and its partners in the region has persisted over thirty-five years since the Khomeini revolution in 1979.

These objectives cannot be viewed in isolation. For example, should ISIS solidify its gains in the region, it could not only generate an ability to mount larger-scale terrorist attacks beyond the region, but also destabilize local oil and gas producing states.

Armed with nuclear weapons, Iran could prove an even more aggressive supporter of terrorism than it has been to date. Moreover, it could also be emboldened to increase its efforts to subvert the governments of regional U.S. partners. Over time a nuclear-armed Iran could threaten vast devastation to the region's oil and gas economic infrastructure, as well as to U.S. and allied military forces operating in the Middle East. Should Iran

[1] I would like to acknowledge the very helpful research support provided by Sean Cate in the preparation of this testimony.

develop an intercontinental ballistic missile and reduce the size of its nuclear warhead, it could also pose a direct threat to the U.S. homeland.[2]

As I will elaborate upon presently, a nuclear-armed Iran could create a structurally unstable nuclear balance with the region's only current (albeit undeclared) nuclear power, Israel. The balance would likely become even less stable should other states in the region follow Iran's path. With this in mind, my testimony first provides an overview of current Israeli and Iranian capabilities, both in terms of weaponry and delivery systems. Second, it offers some observations on the nuclear doctrine both Israel and Iran might adopt. This is followed by my assessment of the prospective characteristics of a nuclear competition between Israel and Iran, and those of a prospective "n-player" competition should Iran's acquisition of nuclear weapons lead other states in the region to follow suit. My testimony concludes with some thoughts on what this means for the United States, to include the strategic choices we confront.

CURRENT CAPABILITIES AND DOCTRINE[3]

Israel

Motivation, Arsenal and Delivery Systems

Israel began seeking nuclear weapons not long after its formation. As a small country with a small population surrounded by hostile, larger neighbors, Israel's leaders felt they could not count on being able to defeat their enemies in a conventional conflict. Nuclear weapons represented a way to offset a prospective inferiority in conventional forces. The Holocaust also had a substantial impact on the thinking of Israeli leaders of that time (as it still does), and there is a determination that such an abomination should never be allowed to happen again.[4]

Although Israel has been a nuclear power for nearly half a century, it follows a policy of "nuclear opacity." Under this policy, Israel does not admit to having nuclear weapons. As a result, no publically available official statements exist regarding Israel's nuclear doctrine.

Reliable and accurate information about Israel's nuclear arsenal is also difficult to obtain given its highly secretive status. Nevertheless, credible reports generally estimate Israel possesses enough weapons-grade plutonium for one hundred to two hundred nuclear

---

[2] Of course, there would be nothing to stop the Iranians from delivering a nuclear weapon to a major U.S. port in the hold of a cargo ship, a threat that occasionally worried Cold War era planners. While the shock of an attack such as this would be great, the damage caused by detonating a weapon at or below the surface would be far less than optimal.

[3] Those familiar with Israeli and Iranian capabilities may wish to proceed to the section titled, "Regional Response: Implications of a Nuclear Armed Iran."

[4] Jeffery Goldberg, "The Point of No Return," *The Atlantic*, September, 2010, available at http://www.theatlantic.com/magazine/print/2010/09/the-point-of-no-return/308186/.

warheads. Some estimates place Israel's arsenal as high as three hundred nuclear warheads, composed primarily of two-stage thermonuclear devices.[5]

Most of Israel's nuclear weapons are believed to be in unassembled mode, with "fully functional weapons" capable of being constructed "in a matter of days."[6] Israel is assessed to possess a "triad" of delivery systems that includes nuclear-capable F-16I fighters, road-mobile Jericho ballistic missiles with estimated ranges of 1,800–3,000 miles (depending on the variant),[7] and five German-built diesel-powered Dolphin-class submarines (with one more on order).[8]

Doctrine

Israeli national security decision-makers since the late 1960s have conceived Israel's nuclear arsenal solely as a deterrent against existential threats, and not as war-fighting instruments or means of coercion.[9] Israel's nuclear doctrine likely remains one of "defensive last resort," with procedural safeguards in place to minimize the risk of accidental or unauthorized use.[10]

That said, due to its lack of strategic depth and small population, Israeli military doctrine has emphasized preemption, preventive action, and fighting on enemy territory. How this would translate to nuclear doctrine against a regional power with nuclear weapons remains to be seen. To date the Israeli Defense Force (IDF) has relied on its conventional superiority to defeat its adversaries, with nuclear weapons assuming the role of "weapons of last resort" to be employed only if the country's very existence were at risk. Should Iran acquire nuclear weapons and Israel judge that such capabilities pose an existential threat, the IDF's nuclear forces could assume a substantially greater role in the country's defense planning.

---

[5] International Institute for Strategic Studies (IISS), "Analysts: Israel viewed as world's 6th nuclear power," *AFP*, April 10, 2010, available at: http://www.iiss.org/whats-new/iiss-in-the-press/april-2010/israel-viewed-as-worlds-sixth-nuclear-power-analysts/. See also Goldberg, "The Point of No Return."

[6] IISS, "Analysts: Israel viewed as world's 6th nuclear power."

[7] "Jericho 1/2/3 (YA-1/YA-3/YA-4)," in, *Jane's Strategic Weapon Systems* (London: IHS Jane's, 2012); and "Israel Test-Fires Nuclear-Capable Ballistic Missile," *Press TV*, September 8, 2013, available at: http://www.presstv.ir/detail/2013/07/13/313543/israel-test-fires-nuclearcapable-missile/; and "Jericho 1/2/3 (YA-1/YA-3/YA-4)," in, *Jane's Strategic Weapons Systems* (London: IHS Jane's, 2015).

[8] Robert Farley, "Nukes on the High Seas: Israel's Underwater Atomic Arsenal," *The National* Interest, October 9, 2014, p. 1, available at http://nationalinterest.org/feature/nukes-the-high-seas-israels-underwater-atomic-arsenal-11434; and Barbara Opall-Rome, "Israel Inaugurates 5th Dolphin-Class Sub," *Defense News*, April 29, 2013, available at: http://www.defensenews.com/article/20130429/DEFREG04/304290008/Isra-el-Inaugurates-5th-Dolphin-Class-Sub.

[9] Avner Cohen, "Nuclear Arms in Crisis under Secrecy: Israel and the Lessons of the 1967 and 1973 Wars," in Peter R. Lavoy, Scott D. Sagan, and James J. Wirtz, eds., *Planning the Unthinkable: How New Powers Will Use Nuclear, Biological, and Chemical Weapons* (Ithaca, NY: Cornell University Press, 2000), pp. 123–124.

[10] Avner Cohen and Marvin Miller, "Bringing Israel's Bomb out of the Basement," *Foreign Affairs*, September/October 2010, p. 39.

Command and Control: Authority

Command authority for the use of nuclear weapons almost certainly rests with the prime minister. However, specific lines of authority are not known.[11] One report states "Israel has an elaborate civilian-controlled [command-and-control] C2 system, which requires three layers of approval to be activated."[12] The one instance where there is publically available information on Israeli considerations of nuclear weapons use involves the 1973 Yom Kippur War. The accounts make it clear that the final decision was then Prime Minister Golda Meir's.[13]

Command and Control: Early Warning

Israel has advanced, networked command-and-control systems that are linked by satellite, fiber, and radio communications. Some command-and-control centers, such as the Israeli Air Force's operational command bunker in Tel Aviv, are believed to be hardened to withstand nuclear attack.[14]

Israel has an extensive early warning system that is integrated with its ballistic missile defenses. Its Elta Green Pine early warning and fire control radar for the Arrow anti-missile system can track targets out to 500 km. The U.S.-controlled AN/TPY-2 radar deployed to Israel has a detection range of over 4,500 km against ballistic missiles and can detect a launch from Iran within seconds. However, the U.S. controls this facility and shares the information it provides with Israel at its discretion. The Israeli military does operate its own reconnaissance satellites, some of which may be able to provide early warning, and it has modern airborne early warning and control aircraft.[15]

---

[11] Bennett Ramberg, "Wrestling With Nuclear Opacity," *Arms Control Today*, The Arms Control Association, November 4, 2010, available at http://www.armscontrol.org/act/2010_11/BookReview.

[12] Shahram Chubin, *Command and Control in a Nuclear-Armed Iran*, Proliferation Papers No. 45 (Paris: Institut Français des Relations Internationale, 2013), available at http://www.ifri.org/sites/default/files/atoms/files/pp45chubin.pdf.

[13] Jeffrey Lewis, "Israel, Nuclear Weapons and the 1973 Yom Kippur War," *Arms Control Wonk*, October 21, 2013, available at http://lewis.armscontrolwonk.com/archive/6909/israel-nuclear-weapons-and-the-1973-yom-kippur-war.

[14] "Israel: Upgraded Air Force command center can withstand nukes," *I24News*, December 14, 2014, available at http://www.i24news.tv/en/news/israel/diplomacy-defense/54399-141214-israel-new-air-force-command-center-can-withstand-nukes.

[15] "Arrow 2 Theatre Ballistic Missile Defense System, Israel," *Army-Technology*, accessed February 17, 2015 at http://www.army-technology.com/projects/arrow2/arrow23.html; Karl Vick and Aaron J. Klein, "How a U.S. Radar Station in the Negev Affects a Potential Israel-Iran Clash," *Time*, May 30, 2012, available at http://content.time.com/time/world/article/0,8599,2115955,00.html; "CAEW Conformal Airborne Early Warning Aircraft, Israel," *Airforce-Technology*, accessed February 16, 2015 at http://www.airforce-technology.com/projects/caew/; "Israel—Air Force" *Jane's World Air Forces*, IHS Jane's; and Brian Berger, "Israeli Rocket Launches Radar Reconnaissance Satellite," *Space News*, April 10,2014, available at http://spacenews.com/40170israeli-rocket-launches-radar-reconnaissance-satellite/.

Iran

Motivation and Delivery Systems

Iran's rationale for seeking nuclear weapons has several possible elements, none of which preclude the others. One is regime preservation in the face of a hostile superpower in the form of the United States, a nuclear-armed enemy in Israel, Sunni Arab rival states, and a neighbor, Turkey, which aspires to expand its influence in the region. Yet Iran could also seek nuclear weapons to support its revisionist goal of reordering the regional geopolitical order with itself at the head, bolstering the regime's sagging domestic legitimacy. Nuclear weapons could enable Tehran to increase its efforts to coerce other states and to expand its support for proxies with less fear of reprisals.

At least initially, Iranian nuclear weapons are likely to rely on a simple design. Such a device would resemble first-generation implosion devices and have a low yield of around 20 kt (slightly more than the Trinity test shot conducted by the United States on July 16, 1945) and a weight of about 1,000 kg (or 2,200 pounds).[16] According to some estimates, Iran probably has enough low-enriched uranium to make seven such weapons upon further enrichment, and it could enrich enough additional material for one bomb every two months. Should Iran's supreme leader give authorization, it could likely convert sufficient low-enriched uranium to high-enriched uranium and assemble a bomb within a year.[17]

What can be stated with a high degree of confidence is that, in addition to its efforts to produce plutonium and enrich uranium to weapons-grade levels, Iran has also been purchasing or developing and fielding delivery systems that would likely comprise part of an overall nuclear force posture. Principal among these capabilities are its ballistic missiles. It seems unlikely, however, that Iran has the financial means, requisite technology, or sufficient skilled manpower to field, man, and maintain a state-of-the art early warning and command and control network of the kind required to deal effectively with the highly compressed warning times associated with an Israeli ballistic missile nuclear attack.

---

[16] "Iran's Nuclear Timetable," *Iran Watch*, December 2, 2014, available at http://www.iranwatch.org/our-publications/articles-reports/irans-nuclear-timetable; and Abdullah Toukan and Anthony Cordesman, *Iran's Nuclear Missile Delivery Capability* (Washington, DC: Center for Strategic and International Studies, 2014), pp. 5, 10.

[17] Based on the calculation that it could produce a 20 kt yield using 16 kg of highly enriched uranium. "Iran's Nuclear Timetable," *Iran Watch;* and Thomas B. Cochran and Christopher E. Paine, *The Amount of Plutonium and Highly-Enriched Uranium Needed for Pure Fission Nuclear Weapons* (Washington, DC: Natural Resources Defense Council Inc., 1995) Table 1, available at https://www.nrdc.org/nuclear/fissionw/fissionweapons.pdf; "Iran's Nuclear Timetable," *Iran Watch;* and Julie Pace, "Obama says Iran at least a year from getting bomb," *The Boston Globe*, October 7, 2013, available at http://www.bostonglobe.com/news/nation/2013/10/07/obama-says-iran-year-more-from-getting-bomb/MNBOHNW4ffkvONE24hRp1L/story.html. Although the last estimate is somewhat dated, it probably reflects the time for Iran to convert its low enriched uranium to highly enriched uranium and weaponize it, rather than any fixed timeline along which Iran may be proceeding.

Based on Tehran's recent and ongoing military efforts, an initial Iranian nuclear force would probably rely heavily on road-mobile ballistic missiles, such as the Shahab 3, as the principal form of delivering nuclear weapons to targets in Israel.[18] At least some of Iran's ballistic missiles are placed in underground silos. Others are kept on transporter/erector launchers (TELs) concealed in caves and bunkers.[19] It is unlikely that Iran has the ability to produce a warhead small enough to fit on a cruise missile. Since Iran's existing missile forces do not appear accurate enough to destroy hardened or buried targets (e.g., missile silos),[20] Tehran's initial nuclear weapons would likely be targeted against "soft" counterforce (e.g., unhardened naval and air bases) and especially countervalue (e.g., population and economic infrastructure) targets. It would also appear likely that, at least initially, Israel would be the primary and perhaps exclusive target of Iran's nuclear forces, although targets in Saudi Arabia and other Gulf states, as well as U.S. military bases in the region could also be placed at risk.

Doctrine

Given Tehran's repeated declarations that it is not developing nuclear weapons, there is nothing in the public domain in the way of an official statement as to what its nuclear doctrine might be.

Command and Control: Authority

There is little information on Iranian command and control systems, let alone on what a prospective Iranian nuclear command and control system might look like. There are reports of Iran recently fielding indigenously produced tactical command and control systems that can integrate command and control centers and early warning, air defense, and missile strike systems. These could be linked via fiber/wired and wireless connections to multi-layered communications networks that provide short-, medium-, and

---

[18] Iran has fourth generation fighters, such as F-14s and MiG-29s. However, without aerial refueling, they would be unable to reach Israel with a nuclear bomb payload (although they could be sent on a one-way "suicide" mission or attempt to recover in Lebanon or Syria). They would also likely be highly vulnerable to Israel's air defenses.

[19] The United States Institute of Peace, "US Intel Assessment," in, *The Iran Primer* (Washington, DC: United States Institute of Peace, 2014), available at http://iranprimer.usip.org/blog/2014/feb/01/us-intel-assessment; and Michael Connell, "Iran's Military Doctrine," in, *The Iran Primer* (Washington, DC: United States Institute of Peace, n.d.), accessed on February 15, 2015 at http://iranprimer.usip.org/resource/irans-military-doctrine

[20] The mainstay of Iran's long-range missile force is currently the Shahab 3, which is inertially guided and believed to have a circular error probable, or CEP, of roughly 8,000 feet (1.5 miles), although some analysts believe it may be as low as 600 feet. This means that Shahab 3 missiles will land within this distance (i.e., between 600-8,000 feet) of their target 50 percent of the time. When delivering nuclear weapons, this degree of accuracy is "good enough" for large, "soft" targets like cities or airbases. Destroying underground bunkers and missile silos, however, requires a much higher degree of accuracy or significantly higher-yield weapons. "Shahab 3," Missile Threat, available at: http://missilethreat.com/missiles/shahab-3/; and "Shahab-3/Zelal-3," Federation of American Scientists, October 1, 2013, available at: http://www.fas.org/programs/ssp/man/militarysumfolder/shahab-3.html.

long-range encrypted communications. Iran also has a network of underground command and control facilities.[21]

Command and Control: Early Warning

Iran's early warning system appears incapable of providing reliable detection of low-observable aircraft; however, it is assessed to be effective against fourth generation fighters. Most notably, three long-range early warning radars have been constructed in the past few years—two Ghadir radars with 1,000 km ranges and one Sepehr radar with a 3,000 km range. They provide 360-degree coverage of the entire country and significant coverage of the region. Tehran claims these radars can detect and identify aircraft, cruise missiles, ballistic missiles, and low-altitude satellites. There is an additional network of twenty-four shorter-range early warning radars located throughout the country.[22] Assuming these capabilities function "as advertised," Iran could have warning of a ballistic missile strike or non-stealthy cruise missile strike.

REGIONAL RESPONSE: IMPLICATIONS OF A NUCLEAR ARMED IRAN

A Bipolar Nuclear Balance

Should Iran acquire a nuclear capability, any assumption that mutual deterrence and strategic stability could be established between Iran and Israel along the lines of that which characterized the U.S.-Soviet Cold War competition should be viewed with skepticism. Based on the historical record of the Cold War and the circumstances in which Iran and Israel would find themselves, a nuclear competition between them will not necessarily curb risk-taking. There are several instances during the Cold War where one protagonist greatly miscalculated the other's willingness to take such risks.[23] Moreover, there is no compelling evidence that Iranian and Israeli leaders have a clear sense of how the other side calculates cost, benefit, and risk—the factors that form the basis of a deterrent posture. Nor does it seem likely at this point that they would engage in confidence-building measures to promote such an understanding if Iran were to field a nuclear weapons capability.

Israel's lack of strategic depth presents it with an enduring and supreme vulnerability, fundamentally different the vast territorial depth enjoyed by both the United States and

---

[21] Sara Rajabova, "Iran unveils new command, control systems," *Azernews*, May 26, 2014, available at http://www.azernews.az/region/67421.html; "Iran unveils new air defense command systems," *Trend*, May 26, 2014, available at http://en.trend.az/iran/2278250.html; and William J. Broad, "Iran Shielding Its Nuclear Efforts in a Maze of Tunnels," *The New York Times*, January 5, 2010, available at http://www.nytimes.com/2010/01/06/world/middleeast/06sanctions.html?pagewanted=all&_r=0.

[22] "Sealing off skies: Iran finalizes 360 degree early warning air defense radar," *RT*, February 15, 2015, available at http://rt.com/news/232515-iran-sepehr-radar-installed/; and Joseph S Bermudez, Jr., "More long-range Iranian early-warning radars revealed," *IHS Jane's 360*, September 4, 2014, available at http://www.janes.com/article/42794/more-long-range-iranian-early-warning-radars-revealed; and Sean O'Connor, "Strategic SAM Deployment in Iran," *Air Power Australia*, April, 2012, available at http://www.ausairpower.net/APA-Iran-SAM-Deployment.html#mozTocId484494.

[23] The October 1962 Cuban Missile Crisis is perhaps the best example of risk-taking that brought the two nuclear powers perilously close to nuclear war.

Soviet Union during the Cold War. In terms of a nuclear strike, Israel has been described as a "one-bomb" country. While this may be an overstatement, a few nuclear detonations over cities like Tel Aviv and Haifa would represent the end of Israel as a viable state. Of course, in the event of such an attack Iran could count on being subjected to a devastating Israeli nuclear counterstrike. Thus Iran in principle would be deterred from initiating a nuclear conflict. Again, however, it is not clear how Iran's leaders would view nuclear weapons use. For example, former Iranian president Hashemi Rafsanjani argued that, "One nuclear bomb inside Israel will destroy everything, [but Israel's retaliation] . . . will only harm the Islamic world. It is not irrational to contemplate such an eventuality."[24]

Considering its inability to absorb even a limited nuclear attack of a half dozen or so warheads and the limitations of ballistic missile defenses, Israel will likely seek to maintain as long as possible the option of executing a decisive, preemptive nuclear attack against Iran's nuclear arsenal if it believes an attack is imminent. Israeli leaders recognize that a first strike against Iran would likely be met with universal condemnation from the international community. Nevertheless, if the very survival of the state of Israel were at stake, then the costs of failing to execute a first strike would likely be viewed as far exceeding the benefits of exercising restraint. Accordingly, Israeli decision-makers will have strong incentives to pursue a counterforce capability in addition to a countervalue ("assured destruction") capability. Yet Iran's mobile missile launchers would very likely present significant challenges to Israeli efforts at counterforce targeting. The Israelis' problems could be further compounded if the Iranians hide some missiles in underground shelters, or acquire the technology to deploy nuclear-tipped cruise missiles at sea. As Iran's nuclear arsenal becomes more survivable through their growing numbers and/or diversification of delivery systems, the challenges associated with Israel maintaining a preemptive nuclear posture would only worsen.

Even assuming both Israel and a nuclear-armed Iran would seek to avoid nuclear use, geographic realities combined with missile speed may conspire to undermine their efforts. Ballistic missile flight times between the two countries are so short that even advanced early warning and command and control systems are likely to be inadequate to enable their leaders to have confidence that they can confirm the attack, decide upon an appropriate response, and issue the commands for executing the response. The problem may not be acute in the course of day-to-day or steady state activities; however, in the event of a crisis, these factors may create an incentive to strike first.

The short warning times could pressure both sides to adopt a heightened alert status, especially in a crisis. Israel could choose to do so in order to preserve the option of launching a decisive pre-emptive first strike, while Iran would do so to avoid becoming the victim of such an attack. To the extent either side seeks to resolve the problem by placing its forces on a hair-trigger alert or extending nuclear release authority to lower

---

[24] Thomas C. Reed and Danny B. Stillman, *The Nuclear Express* (Minneapolis, MN: Zenith Press, 2009), p. 298.

commands, the risk of accidental launch or miscalculation would inevitably increase, especially during a crisis.

The prospects for avoiding nuclear use might be enhanced if, over time, both Israel and Iran fielded secure second-strike forces capable of inflicting assured destruction.[25] Yet even after both the United States and the Soviet Union accumulated vast numbers of nuclear weapons during the Cold War, fears continued to persist on both sides regarding their vulnerability to a disarming first strike.

An "N-State" Nuclear Competition?

It is possible—perhaps even likely—that Iran's acquisition of a nuclear capability would not only produce a nuclear competition with Israel, but also prompt other states in the region to acquire nuclear weapons, creating a multipolar, or "n-state," nuclear competition. While the path toward a nuclear capability has historically been long and arduous, this may not be the case in the wake of Iran's ascension to nuclear power status. Such a shock to the nonproliferation regime could, in fact, precipitate its collapse. Saudi Arabia might exercise what some believe to be a standing option to acquire nuclear weapons from Pakistan or base Pakistani nuclear weapons on its territory with Riyadh exercising de facto control.[26] Or nuclear proliferation might occur on an accelerated schedule, with designs, components, and even fissile material—everything but an assembled warhead itself—being provided on an "installment plan" in a market where the barriers to transfer have all but collapsed.[27]

---

[25] Assured destruction as defined here refers to the ability to inflict casualties and economic damage against a state such that it is annihilated as a functioning entity.

[26] Saudi King Abdullah stated, "If Iran developed nuclear weapons . . . everyone in the region would do the same." A similar statement was made by Prince Turki al-Faisal, former head of Saudi Arabia's General Intelligence Directorate. In 2012, a senior Saudi source declared, "There is no intention currently to pursue a unilateral military nuclear program but the dynamics will change immediately if the Iranians develop their own nuclear capability. . . . Politically, it would be completely unacceptable to have Iran with a nuclear capability and not the kingdom." On the persistent but unconfirmed reports of a Saudi-Pakistani nuclear connection, see Naser al-Tami-ni, "Clear or Nuclear: Will Saudi Arabia Get the Bomb?" *Al Arabiya*, May 21, 2013, available at: http://english.alarabiya.net/en/News/middle-east/2013/05/21/Will-Riyadh-get-the-bomb-.html. See also *Chain Reaction: Avoiding a Nuclear Arms Race in the Middle East*, Report to the Committee on Foreign Relations, United States Senate (Washington, DC: Government Printing Office, 2008), pp. ix, 12, 20; and Ibrahim al-Marashi, "Saudi Petro-Nukes? Riyadh's Nuclear Intentions and Regime Survival Strategies," in William C. Potter and Gaukhar Mukhatzhanova, eds., *Forecasting Nuclear Proliferation in the 21st Century, Vol. II: A Comparative Perspective* (Stanford, CA: Stanford University Press, 2010), pp. 77–78.

[27] Take the example of what Pakistan alone has provided and could provide to accelerate the rate of proliferation. It has, via the A.Q. Khan network, seeded parts of the developing world with nuclear weapon designs and key components (e.g., centrifuges). See *Nuclear Black Markets: Pakistan, A.Q. Khan and the Rise of Proliferation Networks: A Net Assessment* (London: International Institute for Strategic Studies, 2007). See also David Albright, *Peddling Peril: How the Secret Nuclear Trade Arms America's Enemies* (New York: Free Press, 2010). Moreover, Pakistan's projected production of plutonium will far exceed its projected arsenal's requirements. There are reports that Pakistan may have completed a second nuclear plutonium production reactor (Khushab-II) near Khushab, which is the site of the country's first plutonium production reactor (Khushab-I). A third reactor, Khushab III, is under construction. The two reactors are estimated to produce roughly 22 kg of plutonium a year, enough for 10 nuclear weapons. Assuming the third reactor is similar in design to the second (which it appears to be), within a few years Pakistan will be producing enough plutonium for thirty or more nuclear weapons each year. Paul K. Kerr and Mary Beth

Despite the uncertainties regarding which path the region will follow toward a multipolar nuclear competition once Iran achieves nuclear-armed status, several things seem clear. First, even if Saudi Arabia, Turkey, and/or Egypt were to follow Iran into the nuclear club, over the near-term, Israel would likely to maintain a dominant position in which its nuclear arsenal and capabilities far outstrip those of its neighbors. Absent a large-scale transfer of nuclear weapons from an established nuclear power to a regional nuclear aspirant, for perhaps a decade or so Israel's arsenal would likely far exceed the combined arsenals of all other nuclear powers in the region both in terms of the numbers of nuclear weapons and their respective yields. While Israel might lose its formidable advantage over time, early on it will likely maintain a very robust preventive strike capability as well as an assured destruction capability, especially considering that its rivals will also likely lack effective air and missile defenses, early warning, and command and control systems. Yet Tel Aviv would also confront the hard reality that still more countries in the region will have the ability, even with only a handful of nuclear weapons, to inflict devastating damage on the Israeli people and their economy.

A "Nuclear Great Game"

Some declared and undeclared nuclear powers, as well as non-nuclear powers that nevertheless have capable civilian nuclear enterprises outside the Middle East, might have strong incentives to assist states in the region seeking to create or enhance their nuclear posture. The region possesses the world's greatest concentration of oil and natural gas, which are critical to global economic growth. The region is a key geostrategic location, with several maritime trade chokepoints such as the Suez Canal, Strait of Hormuz, and Bab el-Mandeb. Given their dependence on oil and natural gas to fuel their economies, the major powers of the developed and developing world have strong incentives to seek access to and influence in that region. In a proliferated Middle East, this could be achieved in a number of ways, to include assisting local states' efforts to develop a nuclear weapons program, enhancing their existing nuclear forces, and/or providing competing nuclear security guarantees, any of which could further destabilize the region.

This could result in a latter-day "Nuclear Great Game" where states external to the region compete for power and influence within it. In such an environment there could be many potential suppliers of nuclear weapons-related technology. Not all extra-regional suppliers would necessarily have a strong interest in regional stability. Major oil and gas exporters outside the region, Russia in particular, could potentially benefit from the corresponding increase in oil and gas prices that would accompany instability. Thus

---

Nikitin, *Pakistan's Nuclear Weapons: Proliferation and Security Issues* (Washington, DC: Congressional Research Service, June 2012), pp. 5–6, 26–27. See also Christopher Clary and Mara E. Karlin, "The Pak-Saudi Nuke, and How to Stop It," *American Interest*, July–August 2012, pp. 24–31.

Moscow may be far less concerned about the consequences of its actions on regional stability.[28]

Among the technologies and capabilities that are likely to be in highest demand by new nuclear powers in the region are those related to warhead miniaturization and precision guidance, missile defenses, and various forms of intelligence (e.g., early warning; rival force development), while thermonuclear weapons, MIRV technology, depressed trajectory ballistic missiles, and missile-carrying submarines are apt to be accorded lesser priority.

Even those states with an interest in stability may not act in their own best interests. States have been prone to act in ways that value narrow, short-term interests at the expense of more important long-term interests.[29] For example, states like Pakistan or North Korea that are financially strapped may act primarily out of an immediate need for revenue and discount heavily the longer-term consequences of their actions on regional stability and even their own long-term security. Nor can China be counted upon to exercise restraint, given its history of enabling nuclear programs in North Korea and Pakistan.[30]

Perhaps most worrisome from Washington's perspective, the opportunities for other powers to displace its influence could increase dramatically if the United States (and perhaps its allies as well) were to withhold military support for nuclear-armed states in an effort to shore up the NPT regime. Should these efforts fail the United States could end up in the worst of both worlds: failing to achieve its nonproliferation goals while also losing influence with regional nuclear powers to extra-regional rivals.

The "N-State" Competition and Crisis Stability

In a Middle Eastern "n-player" competition, all nuclear powers would be challenged to establish an "assured destruction" capability against all the other regional nuclear powers—another Cold War desideratum—given their relatively modest economies. An "assured destruction" capability in an "n-state" competition would require that each state have weapons sufficient to survive an initial attack by *all* potential rivals and still be able to devastate the countries of *all* potential attackers. It would also require that the source of the attack be reliably identified. This may prove difficult given likely limitations on these states' ability to field advanced early warning systems. For example, would Saudi Arabia be able to determine with confidence the perpetrator of a ballistic missile

[28] This is not to say that Russia would seek to promote a nuclear war, or even a nuclear crisis. Yet, as has been described above, political leaders are not always the masters of events once they are put in motion.

[29] For example, in the nuclear competition alone, China's support for Pakistan's nuclear program appears to be a case of pursuing short-term geopolitical gains at the expense of potentially far greater long-term problems, as described in this paper. Arguably, the U.S. pursuit of multiple independently targetable reentry vehicles (MIRV) technology, rather than first attempting to ban it through arms control agreements, proved short sighted, as it ultimately worked to the relative benefit of the Soviet Union, whose far larger ballistic missiles could accommodate more warheads than their U.S. counterparts.

[30] See Reed and Stillman, *The Nuclear Express*, pp. 328–29.

launched from a location along the Iranian-Turkish border? The origin of any cruise missile launched from a sea-based platform? Even assuming a state could identify the source (or sources) of an attack, could its command and control systems survive the attack sufficiently intact to execute a retaliatory strike? A decapitation strike could preclude an "assured destruction" retaliatory strike even if sufficient weapons survive to execute one.

This, in turn, raises the possibility of a "catalytic" war—one that is initiated between two states by a third party. Given a proliferated Middle East as described here, the chances that a regime would incorrectly attribute the source of an attack cannot be easily dismissed. To the extent cyber weapons could be employed to introduce false information into a state's decision-making process, the risks of catalytic war only increase.

Further complicating matters, the early warning requirement following a proliferation cascade could be multidirectional, and at some point perhaps 360 degrees, especially if multiple nuclear rivals deploy a portion of their nuclear forces at sea. Early warning requirements would be stressed even further if an adjacent state (e.g., Saudi Arabia in the case of Iran) were to acquire nuclear weapons. In this case warning times would be even more compressed than in an Israeli-Iranian competition. Owing to its proximity to Iran, Saudi Arabia, for example, could have less than five minutes to react to a suspected Iranian ballistic missile attack no matter how advanced its early warning and command and control systems.

As noted earlier, regardless of what assumptions are made with respect to a regional nuclear power's early warning system, given the short ballistic missile flight times, it seems likely that preserving command and control of the state's nuclear forces while under attack will prove challenging. States might be tempted to adopt a launch-on-warning posture, but this requires both early warning and a highly responsive command and control system. Should a state determine that it will not be able to launch-on-warning and instead attempt to "ride-out" a nuclear first strike and retaliate, it would still need its command and control system to function effectively in the wake of the nuclear attack. Absent a highly resilient command and control system, a state's ability to launch a retaliatory nuclear strike may require nuclear release authority to be diffused to lower-level commanders. But again, absent an effective early warning system it may not be possible to determine the attack source with confidence in a region with multiple nuclear powers.

Finally, a state could forego a prompt counterstrike in favor of responding days or even weeks following an attack. In theory there is no reason why a nuclear counterstrike would have to be prompt if it were focused solely on punishing the attacker through strikes on counter-value targets. Following this line of reasoning, a regime could hide its nuclear weapons and launchers, recover them in the days following an attack, and launch its retaliatory blow once its surviving nuclear forces had been reconstituted.

While this "buried bomb" posture might be appealing in the abstract, there are significant potential drawbacks that must be addressed. First, the country adopting this posture would have to be able to identify the source of the attack. Second, depending upon the attacker's nuclear arsenal, a time delay may enable a follow-on strike. Third, there would always be a risk that the buried bombs would be located and destroyed in the initial attack or in the follow-on strike. Fourth, the nuclear weapons might even be physically seized by the attacker's conventional or special operations forces following the first strike during what would almost certainly be a period of widespread disorder in the state that had been attacked. Fifth, a coherent command and control system would need to be maintained, not only during the minutes or hours immediately following an attack, but also for days or weeks. Failing that, the state's leadership would likely have to devolve nuclear release authority to lower commands. While this could enhance the prospects of a successful buried bomb retaliatory strike, it would almost certainly increase the risks of an unauthorized or accidental use of nuclear weapons.

SOME IMPLICATIONS FOR U.S. POLICY AND FORCE POSTURE

Given the current state of Iran's nuclear program, the immense resources Iran's leaders have invested in it, the great lengths to which they have gone to deceive the international community regarding their nuclear program, and the substantial advantages that would accrue to Tehran from possessing nuclear weapons, it seems unlikely that anything short of the threat or use of force would deflect the current regime from its objective. Even if the United States and Iran concluded an agreement on Iran's nuclear program in the coming days or weeks, it seems unlikely to alter Tehran's ultimate aim.

If so, these circumstances would leave the United States and its security partners with two basic strategic choices: compel the Tehran regime through the threat or the use of force to abandon its nuclear weapons program, or prepare to live with whatever nuclear posture Iran chooses to adopt, which could range from a "short sprint" to a nuclear capability; an opaque nuclear posture similar to Israel's; or a declared nuclear capability such as North Korea's or Pakistan's.

I will focus my remarks here on the challenges associated with a nuclear-armed Iran. First, I offer some suggestions as to the kind of analyses we might want to do to help insure that we make the best of what is likely to be a difficult situation. Second, I present some thoughts as to what the character of a nuclear competition in the Middle East might imply for U.S. security policy and strategic force posture.

Before proceeding, however, I want to make clear that crafting a well-designed U.S. policy, strategy, and associated force posture in the wake of Iran becoming a nuclear-armed state would be a formidable task, requiring persistent, focused intellectual effort by skilled strategists, as well as execution by highly skilled diplomats and military leaders.

Determining the appropriate U.S. policy, strategy, and military posture in this regard might be usefully informed by assessments of the following issues:

- Developing as best an understanding as possible regarding how Israel and the region's prospective nuclear powers view nuclear weapons, to include the conditions under which they might be employed and how their decision-makers tend to view costs, benefits, and risks (e.g., What do they value most, such as regime survival? What do most fear? How risk tolerant/risk averse are they? Do their worldviews match ours? Etc.)

- Identifying and evaluating a set of scenarios that address the prospective immediate and long-term consequences of a U.S./allied use of force to preclude Iran from acquiring nuclear weapons.
- Identifying and evaluating a set of scenarios that address a regional bipolar nuclear competition between Israel and Iran, to include potential crisis situations as well as a steady state, long-term competition to include the second-order effects on the region (such as an expanded use of proxy warfare by Tehran).
- Identifying and evaluating a set of scenarios that address the prospective emergence of an "n-state" nuclear competition in the region, to include potential crisis situations as well as a steady state, long-term competition to include the second-order effects on the region (such as in the event external major powers engage in a "Nuclear Great Game" for influence in the region).
- Undertaking an assessment of the implications of these prospective futures for U.S. security interests in the region, as well as our force posture and associated capabilities.

In structuring the kinds of assessments and planning scenarios described above, consideration should be given to a range of key factors shaping the nuclear competition, to include the dynamics of "n-player" competitions, the progressive blurring of the "firebreak" between nuclear and advanced conventional weaponry, and geography, to name a but a few.

The U.S. Nuclear Arsenal and Extended Deterrence

Should Iran acquire a nuclear capability, the United States might look to stretch its nuclear umbrella over friendly states in the Middle East in order to enhance their sense of security and reduce their incentive to obtain their own nuclear weapons. This would likely raise familiar issues regarding the size and composition of the U.S. nuclear arsenal, as well as Washington's credibility.

Let's take the last issue first. During the Cold War, America's NATO allies questioned whether Washington would risk a Soviet nuclear attack on Chicago by retaliating for a Soviet nuclear attack on Bonn. In the event of a nuclear-armed Iran, one might suspect Saudi leaders challenging Washington's willingness to order a nuclear response against Tehran should Riyadh be the target of an Iranian nuclear-tipped missile—particularly if Iran had acquired an ability to strike the United States.

The U.S. ability to assure those countries to which it proposes to offer extended deterrence may also depend to a significant extent on the mix of nuclear weapons in its arsenal. While many other nuclear powers—China and Russia in particular—are investing in advanced nuclear designs, to include weapons with very low yields and more focused effects, the United States has chosen to limit its nuclear weapons inventory to weapons designed during the Cold War. By limiting the range of nuclear response options available to the president, this posture may run a significant risk of weakening the U.S. ability to deter its enemies as well as the credibility of U.S. extended deterrence guarantees to allies and partners.

Given the dramatic reductions in the U.S. nuclear arsenal since the Cold War, questions might also arise as to how thinly America's nuclear umbrella is stretched. New START provides the United States parity with Russia in numbers of strategic nuclear weapons. Moscow, however, has not sought to extend nuclear guarantees to other states, while the United States has done so with its European allies, and other allies such as Japan and South Korea—presumably to counter any threat that might be posed by China and/or North Korea. When the United States had thousands of nuclear weapons, one might discount the matter. With the New START commitment to reduce the arsenal size to 1,550, and with the administration floating proposals to reduce the number further to 1,000, one can understand why those offered shelter under the U.S. nuclear umbrella are beginning to wonder if it leaks. Put another way, the United States has nuclear parity with Russia, but it is also committed to defend allies and partners against nuclear threats posed by China, North Korea, and, prospectively, Iran as well.

Thank you again for the opportunity to share my thoughts on these important issues. I will be happy to respond to any questions you might have to the best of my ability during the discussion period.

About the Center for Strategic and Budgetary Assessments

The Center for Strategic and Budgetary Assessments (CSBA) is an independent, nonpartisan policy research institute established to promote innovative thinking and debate about national security strategy and investment options. CSBA's goal is to enable policymakers to make informed decisions on matters of strategy, security policy and resource allocation. CSBA provides timely, impartial and insightful analyses to senior decision makers in the executive and legislative branches, as well as to the media and the broader national security community. CSBA encourages thoughtful participation in the development of national security strategy and policy, and in the allocation of scarce human and capital resources. CSBA's analysis and outreach focus on key questions related to existing and emerging threats to US national security. Meeting these challenges will require transforming the national security establishment, and we are devoted to helping achieve this end.

Senator SESSIONS. Thank you.
Dr. Kroenig?

STATEMENT OF MATTHEW KROENIG, ASSOCIATE PROFESSOR OF GOVERNMENT AND FOREIGN SERVICE, FIELD CHAIR OF INTERNATIONAL RELATIONS AT GEORGETOWN UNIVERSITY, AND SENIOR FELLOW AT THE ATLANTIC COUNCIL

Dr. KROENIG. Chairman Sessions, Ranking Member Donnelly, members of the committee, thank you for inviting me to participate in this important hearing. I am pleased to be here alongside my distinguished colleagues Andrew Krepinevich, George Perkovich, and Ashley Tellis. I would like to commend the committee for initiating this timely discussion of regional nuclear dynamics.

I have worked closely on nuclear issues both in and out of government for over a decade, and my recent work at Georgetown University and the Atlantic Council has focused increasingly on Russian nuclear capabilities and its implications for the United States and NATO. It is this subject on which I have been invited to speak today. In my opening remarks, I will make several brief points. More detail on each can be found in my written testimony.

First, I will begin with Russia's nuclear capabilities. Along with the United States, Russia is one of the world's foremost nuclear powers. At the strategic level, it possesses a triad of nuclear bombers, intercontinental ballistic missiles, and submarines.

In addition to its strategic forces, Russia retains an arsenal of around 2,000 tactical nuclear weapons for battlefield use. This includes nuclear-armed torpedoes, depth charges, short-range missiles, air-to-surface missiles and bombs, and surface-to-air missiles for use in air defense.

Russia has made the thoroughgoing modernization of its nuclear forces and the development of new nuclear capabilities a national priority, even in difficult economic circumstances. Among the new capabilities is Russia's recent test of an intermediate-range ground launch cruise missile. This development is of particular concern because it is in violation of Russia's commitments under the 1987 Intermediate-Range Nuclear Forces, or INF, Treaty, the only arms control treaty ever to eliminate an entire class of nuclear weapons.

Second, turning to Russian doctrine, it is important to emphasize that, unlike the United States, since the end of the Cold War, Russia has moved nuclear weapons toward the center of its national security strategy. Beginning in the early 2000s, Russian strategists have promoted the idea of "de-escalatory" nuclear strikes.

According to this "escalate to de-escalate" concept, Moscow will threaten or, if necessary, carry out limited nuclear strikes early in a conventional conflict in order to force an opponent to sue for peace on terms favorable to Moscow. In addition, at least as telling as public documents are how military forces actually plan and exercise, and nearly all of Russia's major military drills over the past decade have concluded with simulated nuclear strikes.

In some ways, it is not surprising that Russia, as the conventionally inferior power, would consider the use of nuclear weapons early in a conventional war, as this is essentially the reverse of NATO strategy during the Cold War, when it faced a conventionally superior Soviet Union. Nevertheless, Russia's nuclear capabilities and strategy pose a serious threat to the United States and our allies, which brings me to my third point, the possibility of escalation.

The ongoing conflict in Ukraine is very much a nuclear crisis. Throughout the crisis, President Putin and other high-ranking officials have repeatedly issued thinly veiled nuclear threats. Moreover, these threats have been backed up by an explicit brandishing of Russian nuclear forces at a level we have not seen since the end of the Cold War. The message is clear. The West must not interfere lest things escalate to catastrophic levels.

If the conflict in Ukraine were to escalate or President Putin were to rerun his playbook of hybrid warfare from Ukraine against a NATO member, the United States could find itself in a direct military confrontation with Russia. In the event of such a conflict, Russia will likely issue nuclear threats in a bid to force NATO capitulation, and if on the losing end of a conventional conflict, Moscow may conduct a limited nuclear strike in an effort to de-escalate the conflict. To be sure, these scenarios may not be likely, but nuclear deterrence is, by definition, about unlikely, but possible and terribly dangerous contingencies.

This brings me to my final point, recommendations for U.S. nuclear strategy and posture. So long as nuclear weapons retain such a prominent place in Russian strategy, the United States and NATO must retain a policy of, and a serious capability for, nuclear deterrence. At a minimum, U.S. nuclear doctrine needs to be clear and firm that any use of nuclear weapons against the United States or an ally would result in a nuclear counterstrike.

In addition, the United States should leave on the table the possibility of a nuclear response to a strictly conventional Russian assault against a NATO ally. The reason for eschewing a no first-use policy is not that an early nuclear response would be necessary or automatic, but rather because there is no reason to assure Russia that this would not happen.

Moreover, the possibility of nuclear response to non-nuclear attack has a critical assurance element, as NATO's easternmost neighbors would prefer that any Russian attack be deterred by the threat of nuclear response, rather than needing to wait for a costly and lengthy conventional war of liberation. To make these threats credible, the United States and NATO must maintain a sufficiently large, flexible, and resilient nuclear force, including capable nuclear delivery systems and a supporting infrastructure. I, therefore, urge this body to fully fund the much-needed modernization of this country's nuclear forces and infrastructure as planned.

In addition, the United States should upgrade its homeland and theater missile defense systems. While missile defenses could not meaningfully blunt a large-scale Russian nuclear attack, an upgraded system could better provide a defense against, and thus complicate Russian calculations for, a more limited strike on the United States or its allies.

The United States must also make sure that it has a credible response to any Russian battlefield use of nuclear weapons, and it is not at all clear that it does at present. Yields of strategic warheads may be too large for a credible response to a tactical strike, and their use would risk escalation to a catastrophic strategic nuclear exchange. The B61 gravity bombs in Europe are out of range of potential conflict zones in the East without redeployment and/or refueling, and the aircraft in which they are delivered would be highly vulnerable to Russian air defenses.

American B–52 bombers and nuclear-armed air launch cruise missiles are based in the United States, reducing their utility for deterrence and assurance missions in Europe.

The United States should, therefore, consider additional options to deter Russian nuclear aggression, assure regional allies, and if necessary respond to a limited Russian nuclear strike. The options could include—I will just list them quickly—placing lower-yield warheads on strategic missiles, training European crews to participate in NATO nuclear strike missions, forward basing B61 gravity bombs in Eastern Europe, rotationally basing B–52 bombers and nuclear air-launched cruise missiles in Europe, developing a sea-launched cruise missile, or designating the planned long-range standoff weapon, LRSO, for delivery by both air and sea.

The United States must also convince Russia to return to compliance with the INF [Intermediate-Range Nuclear Forces] Treaty and, if that fails, to prevent Russia from gaining a military advantage from its violation. Washington should, therefore, study the development of new intermediate-range missiles and their deployment to Europe. It should also consider the deployment of cruise missile defenses in Europe to defend against Russian nuclear aggression.

Following through on some of these proposals would reverse U.S. and NATO policy of reducing reliance on nuclear weapons as an objective in and of itself. This policy was justifiable so long as Russia remained cooperative, but given increased Russian nuclear aggression, we no longer have the luxury of reducing reliance on nuclear weapons for its own sake and arguably never did.

Some of these proposals, if adopted, would also run counter to promises made to Russia in the NATO–Russia Founding Act of 1997. But Putin has already violated key provisions of this act, and it would be foolish for the United States to be constrained from taking action necessary for its national security by a document that Russia routinely ignores.

Nuclear weapons are tools of great power, political competition, and they remain the ultimate instrument of military force. With long-dormant tensions among the great powers resurfacing, nuclear weapons will again feature prominently in these confrontations, and the United States must be prepared to protect itself and its allies in these conditions.

I know this committee will help ensure the maintenance of the strong American nuclear forces that have undergirded international peace and security for nearly 70 years.

Thank you for the opportunity to be here today. I look forward to your questions.

[The prepared statement of Mr. Kroenig follows:]

PREPARED STATEMENT BY DR. MATTHEW KROENIG

Chairman Sessions, Ranking Member Donnelly, members of the committee, thank you for inviting me to participate in this important hearing. I am pleased to be here alongside my distinguished colleagues Andrew Krepinevich, George Perkovich, and Ashley Tellis.

I would like to commend the committee for initiating this timely discussion of regional nuclear dynamics. I have worked on nuclear issues both in and out of government for over a decade and, as a professor at Georgetown University and a senior fellow at the Atlantic Council, I have focused increasingly on Russian nuclear capabilities and strategy and its implications for the United States and NATO.[1] It is this subject on which I have been invited to speak today.

I will begin with Russia's nuclear capabilities. Along with the United States, Russia is one of the world's foremost nuclear powers. At the strategic level, it possesses a triad of nuclear bombers, intercontinental ballistic missiles (ICBMs), and submarines.[2] Under the New START Treaty, signed in 2010, Russia has committed to deploying no more than 1,550 strategic nuclear warheads by 2018.[3]

Russia has made the thoroughgoing modernization of its nuclear forces and the development of new nuclear capabilities a national priority even under difficult economic circumstances.[4] Russia is updating its bomber fleet, which will carry a new precision-strike, long-range, nuclear-armed cruise missile. A new generation of nuclear submarines is set to enter service and they are designed to deliver a new, more advanced submarine-launched ballistic missile (SLBM), intended to penetrate enemy missile defenses. Moscow is also developing new silo-based and road-mobile ICBMs capable of carrying warheads with multiple independently-targetable reentry vehicles (MIRVs), also designed to defeat enemy defenses.

In addition, Russia has tested a new intermediate-range, ground-launched cruise missile (GLCM).[5] This development is of particular concern because it is in violation of Russia's commitments under the 1987 Intermediate Range Nuclear Forces (INF) Treaty, the only arms control treaty ever to eliminate an entire class of nuclear weapons.[6] In addition, Russia's RS–26 ballistic missile, although tested at longer ranges, can be operated at intermediate range, providing a technical circumvention of the INF Treaty.

In addition to its strategic forces, Russia retains an arsenal of around 2,000 tactical nuclear weapons for battlefield use.[7] This arsenal includes nuclear-armed: torpedoes, depth charges, short-range surface-to-surface missiles, air-to-surface missiles and bombs, and surface-to-air missiles for use in air defense. Although Russia has not publicized plans to modernize its tactical nuclear forces, it is possible that Russia is also upgrading some of these systems as it modernizes its strategic forces.

Turning next to Russian strategy and doctrine, it is important to emphasize that, unlike the United States, since the end of the Cold War, Russia has moved nuclear weapons toward the center of its national security strategy and military doctrine. In the past, Moscow maintained a nuclear "no first use" doctrine, but this policy was abandoned in the year 2000. Since the early 2000s, Russian strategists have promoted the idea of "de-escalatory" nuclear strikes.[8] According to this "escalate to de-escalate" concept, Moscow will threaten, or, if necessary, carry out, limited nuclear strikes early in a conventional conflict in order to force an opponent to sue for peace on terms favorable to Moscow.[9] Russia's 2000 military doctrine stated that nuclear strikes might be conducted in any situation "critical to the national security" of the Russian Federation.[10] The more expansive language about nuclear preemption was excluded from Russia's most recent public documents, but the idea remains firmly engrained in Russian thinking and some speculate that the language remains in classified annexes.[11]

---

[1] For my recent work in this area, see Matthew Kroenig and Walter Slocombe, "Why Nuclear Deterrence Still Matters to NATO," The Atlantic Council (August 2014), available at *http://www.atlanticcouncil.org/images/publications/Why—Nuclear—Deterrence—Still—Matters—to—NATO.pdf* and Matthew Kroenig, "Facing Reality: Getting NATO Ready for a New Cold War," *Survival: Global Politics and Strategy* (February/March 2015), pp. 49–70.

[2] For more detail on Russia's nuclear forces, see Hans M. Kristensen and Robert S. Norris, "Russian Nuclear Forces, 2014," *Bulletin of the Atomic Scientists*, Vol. 70, No. 2 (2014), pp. 75–85.

[3] New Strategic Arms Reduction Treaty (New START), April 8, 2010, available at *http://www.state.gov/t/avc/newstart/c44126.htm.*

[4] On Russian nuclear modernization, see also Kristensen and Norris, 2014.

[5] Michael R. Gordon, "U.S. Says Russia Tested Cruise Missile, Violating Treaty," *The New York Times*, July 28, 2014.

[6] Treaty Between The United States Of America And The Union Of Soviet Socialist Republics On The Elimination Of Their Intermediate-Range And Shorter-Range Missiles (INF Treaty), December 8, 1987, available at *http://www.state.gov/t/avc/trty/102360.htm.*

[7] Krisetenen and Norris, 2014.

[8] Nikolai N. Sokov, "Why Russia Calls a Limited Nuclear Strike 'de-escalation,'" *Bulletin of the Atomic Scientists*, March 13, 2014, available at *http://thebulletin.org/why-russia-calls-limited-nuclear-strike-de-escalation.*

[9] Ibid.

[10] Military Doctrine of the Russian Federation, 2000, available at *http://igcc.ucsd.edu/assets/001/502378.pdf.*

[11] Elbridge Colby, "Nuclear Weapons in the Third Offset Strategy: Avoiding a Blind Spot in the Pentagon's New Initiative," Center for a New American Security (February 2015), pp. 6,

At least as telling as public documents, however, are how military forces actually plan and exercise. Nearly all of Russia's major military drills over the past decade have concluded with simulated nuclear strikes. [12] Moreover, President Putin himself has personally overseen such nuclear exercises. [13]

In some ways, it is not surprising that Russia, as the conventionally inferior power in relation to the United States and NATO, would consider the use of nuclear weapons early in a conventional war, as this is essentially the reverse of NATO strategy during the Cold War when it faced a conventionally superior Soviet Union. Nevertheless, Russia's nuclear capabilities and strategy pose a serious threat to the United States and should be a cause of concern.

This brings me to my next major subject, the possibility of nuclear escalation. For years, Western analysts assumed that Russia's heavy reliance on nuclear weapons was envisaged in the context of a defensive war, but recent events have shown that these tactics can also be employed as part of an offensive campaign. The ongoing conflict in Ukraine is very much a nuclear crisis. [14] Throughout the crisis, President Putin and other high-ranking officials have repeatedly issued thinly-veiled nuclear threats. Moreover, these threats are backed up by explicit brandishing of Russia's nuclear forces at a level we have not seen since the end of the Cold War. Russia has also reserved the right to deploy nuclear weapons in Crimea and Kaliningrad. [15] The message is clear: the West must not interfere in Russia's invasion of Ukraine lest things escalate to catastrophic levels.

If the conflict in Ukraine were to escalate or President Putin were to rerun his playbook of hybrid warfare from Ukraine against a NATO member, the United States could find itself in direct military confrontation with Russia. In the event of such a conflict, Russia will likely issue nuclear threats in a bid to force NATO capitulation and, if on the losing end of a conventional conflict, Moscow may conduct a limited nuclear strike in an effort to "de-escalate" the conflict.

I will conclude with a discussion of the implications of these developments for U.S. nuclear strategy and posture. So long as nuclear weapons retain such a prominent place in Russian force structure, procurement priorities, doctrine, and political rhetoric, it remains an important deterrence mission for the United States and NATO to retain a policy of, and a serious capability for, nuclear deterrence as a potential instrument for dealing with the remote but calamitous contingency of a military confrontation with Russia.

At a minimum, U.S. nuclear deterrence doctrine needs to be clear and firm that any use of nuclear weapons against the United States or an ally would result in a nuclear counterstrike. In addition, the United States should leave on the table the possibility of a nuclear response to a strictly conventional Russian assault against a NATO ally. The reason for not foregoing this option is not that an early nuclear response would be necessary or automatic, but rather because there is no reason to assure Russia that this would not happen. Moreover, the possibility of nuclear response to nonnuclear attack has a critical assurance element as NATO's easternmost neighbors would prefer that any potential Russian attack be deterred by the threat of nuclear strike, rather than needing to wait for a costly and lengthy conventional war of liberation.

To make these threats credible, the United States must field a sufficiently large, flexible, and resilient nuclear force, including capable nuclear delivery systems and supporting infrastructure. I, therefore, urge this body to fully fund the much-needed modernization of this country's nuclear forces and infrastructure as planned.

In addition, the United States should upgrade its homeland and theater ballistic and cruise missile defense systems. While missile defenses could not meaningfully blunt a large-scale Russian attack, an upgraded system could better provide a defense against, and thus complicate Russian calculations for, a more limited strike on the United States or its allies.

---

available at *http://www.cnas.org/sites/default/files/publications-pdf/Nuclear%20Weapons%20in%20the%203rd%20Offset%20Strategy.pdf.*

[12] Sokov, "Why Russia Calls a Limited Nuclear Strike 'De-escalation.'"

[13] Alexey Nikolsky, "Putin Holds Military Drills to Repel Nuclear Strike," RT, May 8, 2014, available at *http://rt.com/news/157644-putin-drills-rocket-launch/.*

[14] For more on this point, see Kroenig, "Facing Reality."

[15] On Russia's claims about nuclear weapons in Crimea, see Sergei L. Loiko, "Russia Says it Has a Right to Put Nuclear Weapons in Crimea," *Los Angeles Times,* September 15, 2014, available at *http://www.latimes.com/world/europe/la-fg-russia-nuclear-crimea-20141215-story.html.* On Russia's threats to deploy nuclear weapons in Kaliningrad, see Bruno Waterfield, "Russia Threatens NATO with Military Strikes over Missile Defence System," *The Telegraph,* May 3, 2012, available at *http://www.telegraph.co.uk/news/worldnews/europe/russia/9243954/Rus- sia-threatens-Nato-with-military-strikes-over-missile-defence-system.html.*

At the sub-strategic level, the United States must seek to negate Russia's overwhelming battlefield nuclear advantage as this is a major contributing causes to Russia's belief that it can achieve escalation dominance through a limited nuclear strike. Ideally, this would be done through arms control negotiations, but the Russians have refused to discuss the reduction of their tactical nuclear weapons and striking an agreement under current conditions would be extremely challenging.

The United States must make sure, therefore, that it has a credible response to any Russian battlefield use of nuclear weapons and it is not at all clear that it does at present.[16] The yields of strategic warheads may be too large for a credible response to a tactical strike and their use would risk escalation to a catastrophic, strategic nuclear exchange. The B61 gravity bombs in Western Europe are out of range of potential conflict zones in the East without redeployment and/or refueling, and the aircraft on which they are delivered would be highly vulnerable to Russian air defenses. American B–52H bombers and nuclear-armed ALCMs are based in the United States, reducing their utility for deterrence and assurance missions in Europe.

The United States should, therefore, consider additional options to deter Russian nuclear aggression, assure regional allies, and if necessary, respond to a limited Russian nuclear strike. The options could include: placing lower-yield nuclear warheads on SLBMs and ICBMs, training European crews to participate in NATO nuclear strike missions, forward basing B61 gravity bombs in Eastern Europe, rotationally basing B–52 bombers and nuclear air-launched cruise missiles in Europe, and developing a new sea-launched cruise missile, or designating the planned long-range standoff weapon (LRSO) for delivery by both air and sea.

The United States must also convince Russia to return to compliance with the INF Treaty and, if that fails, to prevent Russia from gaining a military advantage from its violation. Washington should, therefore, study the development of new GLCMs and their deployment to Europe. It should also consider the deployment of cruise missile defenses in Europe to defend against Russian nuclear aggression.

Following through on some of these proposals would reverse longstanding U.S. and NATO policy of reducing reliance on nuclear weapons as an objective in and of itself. This policy was justifiable so long as Russia remained cooperative, but given increased Russian nuclear aggression, we no longer have the luxury of reducing reliance on nuclear weapons for its own sake and arguably never did.

Some of these proposals, if adopted, would also run counter to promises made to Russia in the NATO–Russia Founding Act of 1997, but Putin has already violated key provisions of this act, including the commitment to refrain ''from the threat or use of force against . . . any other state, its sovereignty, territorial integrity or political independence in any manner.''[17] It would be foolish for the United States to be constrained from taking action necessary for its national security by a document that Russia routinely ignores.

I know this Committee will help ensure the maintenance of the strong American nuclear forces that have undergirded international peace and security for nearly seventy years.

Thank you again for the opportunity to be here today. I look forward to your questions.

Senator SESSIONS. We got notice that a vote has already started. I am inclined to think that we should just break because your statements are very important, and I would like to hear them. So we will take a break for the vote.

I guess that is the signal that the vote has started. So why don't we just go and make a quick return in 10–12 minutes for one vote. So we will be back.

[Whereupon, at 2:54 p.m., the committee recessed, to reconvene at 3:07 p.m., the same day.]

Senator SESSIONS. Okay, we will reconvene. That was not as long as sometimes it takes. Senator Donnelly and King got their business done and got out of there.

---

[16] For information on U.S. nuclear forces and further details on the items in this paragraph, see Hans M. Kristensen and Robert S. Norris, ''U.S. Nuclear Forces, 2014,'' *Bulletin of the Atomic Scientists* vol. 70, no. 1 (2014), pp. 85–93.

[17] ''Founding Act on Mutual Relations, Cooperation and Security between NATO and the Russian Federation,'' May 27, 1997, available at *http://www.nato.int/cps/en/natolive/official—texts—25468.htm.*

Senator DONNELLY. We have young legs.

Senator SESSIONS. Let us see. Dr. Tellis, thank you for coming again, and now we look forward to hearing from you.

STATEMENT OF ASHLEY TELLIS, SENIOR ASSOCIATE, CARNEGIE ENDOWMENT FOR INTERNATIONAL PEACE

Dr. TELLIS. Chairman Sessions, Ranking Member Donnelly, members of the committee, thank you for the invitation to testify today.

My testimony focuses on a segment of the Asian nuclear space, namely China, India, and Pakistan. My written testimony looks at different dimensions of the nuclear programs in these countries, but in my oral remarks I am going to focus mostly on the drivers that have pushed these countries to modernize their nuclear programs. I want to end by identifying some contingencies that would be of importance to the United States and the challenges for protecting the U.S. strategic deterrent as we go forward.

I would be grateful if you include my written statement into the record.

Senator SESSIONS. We will make all of your statements a part of the record. Thank you.

Dr. TELLIS. Thank you.

Let me start by noting that although China, India, and Pakistan are modernizing their nuclear deterrence comprehensively, only China's nuclear expansion is driven fundamentally by concerns about the United States. China aims to create a nuclear force that is sufficiently immune to both United States nuclear and conventional weapons systems, while also intending to deter direct United States attacks and coercion against China, while contributing to deterring United States intervention on behalf of its allies in any regional crisis, especially in East Asia.

Satisfying these multiple aims requires China to have a substantial and a survivable deterrent, one that is also intended to deter India, Russia, Japan, and other regional powers simultaneously.

India's nuclear program, which historically began in response to China's, is intended today primarily to correct its abject vulnerability, vis-&-vis Beijing, while also deterring Pakistan, India's two principal adversaries. The principal thrust of India's nuclear weapons modernization, therefore, is focused on increasing the range and survivability of its delivery systems primarily to deter China.

Pakistan's nuclear program, which is perhaps the fastest-growing program of the three countries, is aimed, as it has been from the beginning, at checkmating India's conventional superiority. In contrast to both China and India, which view their nuclear weapons primarily as second-strike systems, Pakistan's nuclear doctrine conceives of its weapons as being used first, mainly in response to a conventional attack by India. Hence, Pakistan has invested heavily in developing a diverse set of capabilities ranging from the strategic to the tactical.

The bottom line is that nuclear weapons programs in the greater South Asian region are alive and well and will be so for some time to come.

There are two sets of contingencies that arise from the expansion of nuclear weapons in this part of the world. The Chinese effort to undermine United States extended deterrence in East Asia, especially with respect to Japan, Taiwan, and our other treaty allies, and the risks to nuclear security in Pakistan remain direct threats to the United States.

Pakistan's support for terrorism against India under cover of its nuclear weapons program and the possible employment of nuclear weapons in an Indo-Pakistani or Sino-Indian conflict, while undoubtedly serious dangers, remain indirect threats to United States interests. To my mind, there are three implications for U.S. strategic forces that flow from these realities.

First, U.S. strategic forces remain the ultimate backstop for American security and, hence, must be modernized and maintained at New START numbers, at least at New START numbers, given the prospect of continued nuclear expansion in Asia. In other words, given the onerous United States extended deterrence commitments in Europe and Asia, United States nuclear parity with Russia must not diminish to a point where parity with China appears within reach.

Second, the United States must maintain the requisite superiority of the total force that permits it to achieve conventional success in regional contingencies, while consciously integrating nuclear options into current planning for successful power projection in Asia, especially in the efforts now underway to defeat China's anti-access area denial programs. United States regional allies need the assurance that the growing Chinese nuclear capability will not paralyze the United States or prevent it from coming to their defense in a crisis.

Third, the desire to reduce the salience of nuclear weaponry in global politics is estimable. But that desire should not extend to devaluing the utility of nuclear weapons for deterrence, damage limitation, and sometimes use against difficult conventional targets. Maintaining this balance is admittedly challenging, but successful deterrence inevitably involves the management of difficult and complex contradictions.

Thank you, Mr. Chairman. I will be happy to answer any questions.

[The prepared statement of Dr. Tellis follows:]

Congressional Testimony

CHINA, INDIA AND PAKISTAN—GROWING NUCLEAR CAPABILITIES WITH NO END IN SIGHT

Testimony by **Dr. Ashley J. Tellis**
Senior Associate,
Carnegie Endowment for International Peace

Strategic Forces Subcommittee of the
Senate Armed Services Committee
February 25, 2015

Chairman Sessions, Ranking Member Donnelly and Members of the Subcommittee on Strategic Forces, thank you for the invitation to testify on regional nuclear capabilities and their impact on U.S. security. I will focus my attention today on a segment of the Asian nuclear space, namely China, India, and Pakistan, their strategic interactions, and the impact of their nuclear weapons modernization on each other and on the United States. The nuclear weapon programs in these three countries are worthy of attention because they are active, expanding, and diversifying at a time when the overall global trend remains a continuing contraction of nuclear inventories. As requested by you, Mr. Chairman, my testimony will explore why this is the case and what challenges ensue from such expansion.

China

Unlike India and Pakistan, China is formally a nuclear weapon state under the nuclear Non-Proliferation Treaty (NPT). China is also a major nuclear power possessing advanced, repeatedly tested, and diverse nuclear weapons designs, diverse delivery systems, and a centralized command and control network that is intended to ensure that the leadership of the Chinese Communist Party can exercise effective command of the country's nuclear weaponry.

In contrast to the United States and the former Soviet Union, China historically maintained a small nuclear force consisting primarily of land-based missiles whose warheads were stored separately, with the delivery vehicles maintained routinely in un-alerted status in silos or caves. This relatively relaxed posture was viewed as sufficient to protect Chinese security during the Cold War because Beijing believed that the positive externalities of mutual U.S.-Soviet nuclear deterrence bestowed on China sufficient protection. Because even a small number of survivable nuclear weapons capable of reaching an adversary's homeland could wreak unacceptable damage, Chinese leaders sought to maintain relatively modest forces that through a combination of opacity, sheltering, and sometimes limited mobility, could survive the remote contingencies of direct nuclear attack at a time when these dangers were limited principally by the political constraints of strong bipolar competition.

With the ending of the Cold War and with the progressive rise of Chinese power, Beijing—whether it publicly admits it or not—has come to view the United States as its principal strategic competitor. Given China's recognition of the sophistication of U.S. nuclear and conventional forces in the face of Beijing's desire to reclaim the strategic primacy it once enjoyed in Asia, Chinese nuclear modernization became inevitable. This modernization, which consists principally of efforts to increase the survivability of its nuclear deterrent in the face of what it perceives to be a formidable U.S. nuclear threat supplemented by other major regional dangers from Russia, India, and other prospective nuclear powers, has taken the following form: the deployment of new land-based solid-fueled ballistic missiles of varying ranges (to include intercontinental-range ballistic missiles); ballistic missile submarines with weapons capable of reaching the continental United States; new highly survivable nuclear weapon storage sites; and a robust national command and control system that incorporates a resilient, dedicated nuclear command and control segment.

The number of nuclear warheads in the Chinese arsenal has also progressively increased as the nuclear delivery systems have been augmented, but there still significant uncertainties about the existence and the number of nuclear gravity bombs and tactical nuclear weapons in the Chinese arsenal. The total size of the Chinese nuclear weapons inventory today is widely believed to consist of some 250 nuclear warheads, but the accuracy of these or any other numbers is debatable. China has a substantial fissile material stockpile consisting of some 16 metric tons of highly enriched uranium and some 1.8 metric tons of weapon-grade plutonium, so there are no practical constraints on its ability to produce an arsenal of any size it chooses. Given the choices China makes in regard to delivery systems, it could deploy anywhere up to an additional 150 warheads over the next ten years.

At arsenal levels of such size, the Chinese nuclear force will be oriented fundamentally towards deterring nuclear use (or the threat of use) against China by maintaining a survivable retaliatory capacity during conflicts with any nuclear-armed state and by maintaining the capacity for escalation dominance vis-à-vis weaker nuclear adversaries. Toward these ends, China will continue to reiterate its "no first use" nuclear policy, though what that doctrine means precisely is unclear.

China today views the United States as its principal active nuclear and conventional threat, followed by India in the nuclear realm. Russia remains a latent nuclear threat and although it was historically an important driver of Chinese nuclear planning, Russia has receded considerably in Chinese calculations today. North Korea, Taiwan, and Japan remain longer-term sources of strategic uncertainty for Beijing, with nuclear threats remaining a current or prospective challenge in all three cases. The most pressing practical contingencies involving Chinese nuclear use in the prospective future, however, involve employment against U.S. forces to forestall defeat or signal a willingness to risk further escalation in the context of a successful U.S. intervention in a Taiwan crisis or in another crisis of similar magnitude in East Asia (for example, on behalf of Japan), and the use of tactical (or other) nuclear weapons in a conflict with India.

India

The rivalry between China and India since their birth as modern states after the Second World War created the preconditions for a nuclear rivalry between them—a competition that was inflamed when China first tested nuclear weapons in 1964 driven by its antagonism to the United States and its emerging split with the Soviet Union. The first Chinese nuclear test, coming two years after India's defeat in the 1962 Sino-Indian conflict, precipitated the Indian nuclear weapons program, which in turn first demonstrated its capacity in 1974. Despite the supposed Chinese disdain of India, Beijing began to systematically target India with nuclear weapons after the latter's first nuclear test, and sometime in the late-1980s transferred a nuclear weapon design and fissile material to Pakistan, at least in part as a strategy of containing India. New Delhi responded to the Chinese challenge with additional nuclear tests in 1998, declared itself to be a nuclear weapon state, and began to overtly develop its nuclear deterrent since—aimed at both China and Pakistan.

India today is believed to possess an arsenal of some 100 nuclear weapons, though this figure is highly uncertain. The country is thought to have produced close to 600 kilograms of weapons-grade plutonium, though it is unclear whether all this material has been machined into warheads. India can produce extremely large quantities of weapons-grade plutonium, should it chose to use its power reactors currently outside of safeguards for this purpose. To date, however, there is no evidence that India has embarked on any crash program to enlarge its nuclear arsenal, despite its having the technical capacity to do so. If India persists in producing about 5-6 nuclear weapons annually (as it is believed to have done since 1998), the India nuclear deterrent would consist of some less than 200 nuclear weapons by 2025—assuming the public assessments of its current inventory are correct. These weapons will be deployed aboard primarily mobile, solid-fueled, ballistic missiles of up to intermediate range, though these will be supplemented by a limited number of legacy gravity weapons and a small but growing number of sea-launched ballistic missiles. All Indian nuclear weapons currently are maintained routinely in de-mated condition, though whether this posture will persist after the four ballistic missile submarines are eventually inducted into its arsenal is unclear.

The heart of India—s current nuclear modernization program, which is centered on developing and inducting mobile, sold-fueled intermediate-range ballistic missiles, deploying ballistic missile submarines, developing a ballistic missile defense system, building weapon storage and integration sites, and completing its command and control network, is aimed principally at refurbishing its deterrence capability vis-à-vis China. The threats emerging from Pakistan are significant, but Indian policy makers judge that their current deterrent against Islamabad as generally adequate. The deterrence gap versus China, however, is considerable and it will not be bridged until India acquires the capacity to range the Chinese heartland with missiles of adequate reach.

Even when the effort to reach this goal is completed—an endeavor that will continue well beyond 2025—it is likely that New Delhi will persist with its currently relaxed nuclear posture so long as current trends in Sino-Indian and Indo-Pakistani relations persist. This posture is predicated on the requirement of a —minimum—deterrent (whose numerical size is not publicly known) and a strict —no first use—policy (which is likely to subsist durably because of India—s general conventional military superiority over Pakistan and its still substantial, though decaying, operational military superiority over China along their disputed border). As long as these conditions obtain, there is little incentive for India to violate its —no first use—policy, which is oriented fundamentally towards deterring nuclear attack (or threats of attack) emerging from Pakistan and China.

Pakistan

The contrast between India and Pakistan on "no first use" could not be greater. Unlike India, which is both stronger than Pakistan and no pushover where China is concerned, Pakistan is a weak state that is unfortunately growing even weaker as a result of its awful strategic choices. Pakistan's security competition with India, which dates back to the creation of the two countries as independent states, is multi-dimensional in nature and involves territorial, religious, and power-political dimensions. These grievances have combined in unhelpful ways to make Pakistan the anti-status quo power in the Indian subcontinent. Having fought four unsuccessful wars with India in an effort to secure its strategic aims, Pakistan switched to a dangerous and provocative strategy in the last decades of the 20th century—a strategy of supporting terrorist groups aimed at enervating India through "a thousand cuts," even as Pakistan began to feverishly expand its nuclear arsenal in an effort to prevent New Delhi from retaliating with conventional forces.

The post-2001-02 shift in Indian policy, which holds out the threat of conventional retaliation to Pakistani-supported terrorist attacks (despite the overarching presence of nuclear weapons in the subcontinent), has only deepened Pakistan's dependence on nuclear weapons further, resulting in an acceleration of its weapons program. Today, the Pakistan arsenal includes both gravity weapons and ballistic missiles of up to medium range as well as cruise missiles, glide bombs, and a plethora of new and diverse tactical nuclear weapons. The Pakistani nuclear arsenal is judged by many reputable scholars to consist of some 90-110 weapons, though at the current pace of growth the force could easily expand to over three times that number within a decade.

Pakistan's strategic weaponry is believed to be deployed in de-mated condition routinely in peacetime. Whether that posture will apply to the newer tactical systems is unclear. Pakistan's nuclear doctrine, unlike India or China's, is centered fundamentally on first use, and it is oriented primarily towards defeating India's conventional superiority in the event of conflict. Although Pakistan's nuclear forces are intended, strictly speaking, for deterrence and not war fighting, Islamabad's emerging tactical capabilities could inadvertently push Pakistan towards the latter.

The external dangers of deterrence breakdown, which could precipitate the catastrophe of Pakistani nuclear use against India, are complemented by internal dangers as well. Pakistan's internal fissures, it is often feared, could bleed into its armed forces, resulting in risks to the security of its nuclear weaponry. Although the Pakistani military has made enormous investments in enhancing nuclear security (aided by the United States) in recent years, fears about the loss or compromise of its nuclear weaponry because of domestic dangers still persist—and not unreasonably so.

Taking Stock

When all three states are synoptically considered, therefore, the following contingencies remain the most pressing from the viewpoint of U.S. strategic interests for the reasons adduced below:

1) Chinese use or threats of use of nuclear weaponry to deter U.S. military intervention on behalf or Taiwan or other American allies in Asia.

Of the three nuclear weapons states that are the subject of this testimony, only China conceives of its nuclear arsenal as having direct utility for deterring U.S. military operations directed against its interests at various locations along the Asian rimland. Any contingency that brings U.S. forces in confrontation with China would represent a dangerous predicament and would require both local conventional and overall nuclear superiority for political and military success. Any failure on this score could not only precipitate immediate operational reverses that would frustrate the realization of U.S. political aims, but it could lead over time to the erosion of the U.S. alliance system in East Asia, the future acquisition of nuclear weapons by current American allies, and the eventual loss of American primacy in the Indo-Pacific. For all these reasons, preparing seriously to ensure success in this contingency should remain at the top of American strategic priorities. The recent innovations centered around the "AirSea Battle" concept indicate that the Pentagon has taken the emerging Chinese threats to the U.S. ability to aid its East Asian allies seriously, though it is unclear whether force planning for nuclear escalation vis-à-vis China has been adequately integrated into the current war plans. If this lacuna is real, it could prove costly in the context of a conflict—and could undermine the confidence of the allies in the viability of the U.S. nuclear umbrella.

2) Pakistani "use" of nuclear weapons as cover to support continued terrorist attacks against India.

Although this contingency derives from Pakistan's ability to exploit the deterrence capability inherent in its nuclear reserves for revisionist ends—and represents the dominant threat levied by the Pakistani military against India now for some three decades—it embodies the most likely route to nuclear deterrence breakdown in South Asia. Neither Indian nor U.S. nuclear capabilities are directly useful in defeating this threat, but U.S. and international political pressure on Pakistan, which has been employed episodically, might offer a means of mitigating its worst dangers. The most likely antidote that could alter such Pakistani behavior, however, would be the rising costs of terrorist blowback within Pakistan—which is, unfortunately, an expensive way of getting Pakistan to change course.

3) Pakistani nuclear use against India or against Indian military forces in the context of Indian retaliation against Pakistani-supported terrorist attacks against India.

This contingency arises if India decides to retaliate against Pakistan through the large scale use of military force for punitive purposes. Any significant employment of Indian military force obviously carries the risk of a Pakistani nuclear response, which is why Indian leaders have shied away from exercising major conventional war options that require especially the large scale use of land forces. Should India contemplate major military operations, however, it is likely that the United States would intervene, but mainly through energetic diplomacy as it did in 2001-02 and again in 2008. It is unlikely that the United States would choose to intervene militarily to prevent either conflict escalation or nuclear weapons employment for a host of operational reasons, though some kinds of trans- or post-conflict assistance might be feasible: in such circumstances, the most important U.S. capabilities that would be relevant would be intelligence, surveillance and reconnaissance (ISR) assets, capabilities required for noncombatant evacuation operations, and Nuclear Emergency and Support Teams (NEST) and other assets essential for post-detonation assistance and recovery (if nuclear use has occurred). Because of the large numbers of U.S. citizens normally resident or traveling in India, and the complexity of evacuation operations in a nuclear environment, this scenario can be more stressing than is commonly realized. The most useful U.S. contribution towards preventing a Pakistani use of nuclear weapons in such a scenario—and the Indian nuclear retribution that would result thereafter—would be to press Pakistan to exit the terrorism business or risk being left alone (or, even worse, the object of international sanction) if a major Indian military response ensues in the aftermath of any pernicious terrorist attack. Other than this, there is little that the United States can do to preserve deterrence stability between two asymmetrically-sized states where the gap in power promises to become even wider tomorrow than it is today.

4) Pakistani loss of control over nuclear assets in the context of conventional military operations against India OR a compromise of nuclear security in peacetime in Pakistan.

This scenario, which has been discussed considerably in recent years both in India and in the United States, would also be highly complex in the demands it places on the U.S. military, depending on the details of the contingency. U.S. ISR elements, special operations forces, and other quick reaction capabilities would be highly relevant in such a contingency—as would close coordination with the government of Pakistan and its armed forces. The United States has already aided Pakistan significantly in regards to nuclear weapons protection, but there are obvious limits to further assistance beyond a point, not least because of the deep-rooted Pakistani fears about the United States seeking access and information about the location of Pakistan—s nuclear weaponry.

5) Chinese or Indian nuclear coercion against the other in the context of a border crisis OR in the limiting case, the actual use of nuclear weapons to stave off battlefield defeat.

This last contingency, admittedly remote today, would put a high premium on U.S. ISR assets as well as, obviously, active U.S. diplomacy. At the present, it is unlikely that the United States would find itself involved in such a conflict except as a concerned bystander, but if this situation were to change as U.S.-Indian ties grow deeper over time, U.S. conventional and nuclear forces might acquire new roles for extended deterrence and reassurance with respect to India. Until then, however, U.S. ISR capabilities and diplomacy would represent the instruments most relevant to coping with such a scenario.

Implications for the United States

The broad range of nuclear challenges arising from a consideration of the problems involving China, India and Pakistan suggest several important conclusions as far as U.S. strategic forces are concerned.

First, U.S. nuclear forces will continue to remain the ultimate backstop where American national security is concerned. The notion that these forces will become irrelevant any time soon, or that their abolition can be contemplated, is a dangerous fantasy. Eliminating nuclear weapons globally must instead take a backseat to protecting U.S. nuclear dominance and maintaining the effectiveness of the U.S. nuclear deterrent over the long term.

Second, the progressive growth of Chinese, Indian, and Pakistani nuclear forces over the next ten years—and the likelihood of further proliferation elsewhere in years to come--implies that any further reduction of U.S. nuclear forces beyond the New Start treaty ought to be eschewed. Given the complexity of the emerging nuclear environment—a world that is best described as asymmetric nuclear multipolarity—the United States must seek to maintain the requisite superiority of the total force that permits it to achieve conventional success in regional contingencies while preserving the advantages currently enjoyed by U.S. nuclear forces. Given the onerous U.S. extended deterrence commitments in Europe and Asia, American nuclear parity with Russia must not diminish to a point where parity with China slinks into reach.

Third, the United States must think seriously about the threat of nuclear deterrence breakdown in Asia as a time when the continent will host many nuclear powers whose arsenals vary in capacity, architecture and doctrine. The desire to reduce the salience of nuclear weaponry in global politics is estimable. That means that U.S. nuclear weapons ought not to be brandished unnecessarily. However, it does not imply forgetting that U.S. nuclear weapons are still essential for deterring not only nuclear attacks (or the threats thereof) on the United States and its allies but also major conventional attacks as well, while still remaining useful as tactical warfighting instruments in certain specific, admittedly limited, contingencies where conventional weapons currently remain ineffective. As a general rule, therefore, the desire to reduce the salience of nuclear weapons in world politics should not extend to devaluing the utility of nuclear weapons for deterrence because these instruments will continue to remain the *ultima ratio* in an environment that only promises more, not less, proliferation.

Senator SESSIONS. Thank you very much.
Dr. Perkovich?

STATEMENT OF GEORGE PERKOVICH, VICE PRESIDENT FOR STUDIES, CARNEGIE ENDOWMENT FOR INTERNATIONAL PEACE

Dr. PERKOVICH. Thank you to the chairman and ranking member and Senator King.

I am just going to follow on my friend Ashley's comments because we are both working on Asia and so burrow into them a little bit. In my written testimony, I hit on five themes. Here, I am just going to focus on a couple of them.

The first is to highlight that the threat perceptions and nuclear requirements and policies of the states in Northeast Asia and South Asia are causally linked to each other and to what the United States does. In my written testimony, I have got a diagram of this dynamic here, but I think it is often lost sight of.

You can think of it in terms of two triangles. So you have the United States, Russia, and China in a triangle. The United States benchmarks historically what it needs in terms of what Russia had. More recently, we have been benchmarking our requirements to what China is doing.

China, in turn, calculates what its strategic requirements are in terms of not only United States nuclear capabilities, but also United States cyber capabilities, United States strategic conventional capabilities, and ballistic missile defenses. So they are all feeding off each other, and it is not just nuclear for nuclear.

There is a second triangle, which includes China, India, and Pakistan. So these two triangles meet in China. As Ashley talked about, China is the benchmark for India's requirement, what it needs in terms of nuclear warheads and delivery systems. As already mentioned, though, that target that China presents is being affected by China's effort to balance the United States.

India is also balancing against Pakistan—to deter Pakistan. China is helping Pakistan. So India has got to be thinking about China, Pakistan, and the help that China provides Pakistan.

Pakistan looks at India and calibrates what it needs, but Pakistan is also looking at the United States and India collaborating and say, ''Okay, what we need is also the product of this United States-India collaboration.''

So you have got these two triangles operating in a very keen way, and so I think one take-away for U.S. policymakers and the policymakers in the region is to realize that anything that we or they do, in terms of capabilities or actions, will affect all of the others. That would include force modernization. It is not an argument against doing it, but it is to understand that there will be reverberations beyond China, but into South Asia with whatever is done.

Second point I want to highlight is that—and Ashley referred to it also—the most complicated challenges facing U.S. nuclear policymakers today are about extended deterrence. In particular, reassuring Japan that the United States has the resolve and the capabilities to defend it against armed attack from China or any other threat.

Now, extended deterrence is often conflated with extended nuclear deterrence. They are related, but they are not necessarily the same thing. It is tempting to believe that the potential use of nuclear weapons always strengthens extended deterrence, but the issue is actually problematic, and that is true in Asia as well as in Europe.

Potential use of nuclear weapons in an escalating conflict can indeed strengthen the potency of our guarantee to the countries that we protect. But the very destructiveness that the specter of nuclear weapons portends also can weaken the resolve of our own society and the protégé's society. So the classic line, should we trade Los Angeles for Okinawa? Or if you are in Japan, if the United States uses a nuclear weapon against China, China is going to nuke us.

So this can be divisive and can be exploited by a potential aggressor, and I think we have been seeing this with what Russia has been doing in Ukraine. That you make a nuclear threat to see if you can split either the guarantor from the protégé or weaken the resolve of the protégé. So it is not an automatically positive deterrent effect. It can, in fact, be divisive and a weakening one.

But there is also an opposite problem in extended deterrence. That is if the guarantor's resolve is unquestioned—our resolve in this case—in the face of a countervailing nuclear threat, a nuclear moral hazard may be created. It is like a finance company whose managers believe that the government will bail them out if they get into ruinous losses. The protégé may take risks in its policies towards the adversary, feeling that the nuclear threat that we offer to defend them will bail them out from any crisis. That is a moral hazard.

The other moral hazard, which we also see in finance, is that relying on the magic of nuclear deterrence, our allies may under invest in conventional capabilities. We can save a little money here because we are counting on the nukes to do the trick. That is like banks that do not keep adequate Reserves to cover their commitments. We have seen that historically in NATO, and we have seen it historically with Japan.

So all of this comes together, I believe, in the situation in the Senkaku-Diaoyu Islands, where Japan and China are in a sovereignty dispute over these uninhabited islands, and where there is a potential of crisis or escalation either on purpose or by accident. In 2010, they had two ships collide accidentally. Now, you have got two highly nationalistic, kind of strongmen leaders in both countries, and if you have one of these collisions, it is easy to imagine a potential escalation.

Obviously, you want to do deal with that by diplomacy, but it is worth thinking through the implications of a potential conflict and having the conventional capability to prevent China from being able to change the facts on the ground.

It is a conventional issue that they not be able to set foot on one of those islands and hold it. Because if you have to fight to take it back, and you get into that kind of potentially escalating conflict and we are not prevailing, someone in this town or someplace else is going to say we ought to make a nuclear threat. That is what nuclear deterrence is for.

But then it raises the issue, is it credible or advisable for the United States to think about first use of nuclear weapons, because that is what we are talking about here, over some islands that 99 percent of the U.S. population has never heard of and could not find on a map? It seems to me that is an invitation for a real disaster in terms of U.S. credibility and extended deterrence.

The way to prevent it is with convention capabilities, both ours and the Japanese, and through exercising those capabilities. The current U.S. nuclear posture, in terms of the numbers envisioned in New START, is totally sufficient to deal with that kind of scenario. It is not a nuclear problem.

Last thing I would say is on South Asia, picking up on what Ashley said. Here, I think there really are challenges for U.S. policy that have not been well addressed. The dynamic Ashley is talking about is an unprecedented one, where you have—the conflict starts with a terrorist attack. Then India makes a conventional military response. Pakistan says it would respond with battlefield nuclear weapons. India, which does not have battlefield nuclear weapons, said they will respond with massive retaliation.

There is no theory to deal with that. All the theories of deterrence do not deal with the possibility that terrorism is this thing that starts it. The theories and practices about how you deal with terrorism have never been applied with antagonists with nuclear weapons.

So we are all kind of groping in the dark in this challenge, and I think it would behoove the committee and the Congress and others in the United States Government to ask, if we do get into a situation of a conflict, and the United States detects Pakistan to be preparing nuclear weapons for use against India—where there are a lot of Americans at all times, where American investment is very heavy, we have got a very strong Indian-American population in the United States. You see Pakistan getting ready, what does the United States do?

I do not think we have prepared for that. We have not thought about it. Do you intervene? How? If not, what do you tell India? How do you do it?

If, God forbid, a conflict like that happens, I am willing to bet that the Senate, or the Congress more broadly, will conduct an inquiry to ask: What did the President know? When did he or she know it? What did they do to prevent it?

We are not taking the steps now to analyze how you work back from that kind of scenario. It has nothing to do with U.S. forces. U.S. nuclear forces are irrelevant to this problem, but it is a clear and present problem, I would submit, that ought to be addressed.

Let me stop there. Thank you.

[The prepared statement of Dr. Perkovich follows:]

PREPARED STATEMENT BY DR. GEORGE PERKOVICH

Mr. Chairman, members of the subcommittee, it is an honor to testify before you. I have worked on nuclear-weapons-related issues since 1982, first with a focus on the Soviet Union, then, after 1992, on India, Pakistan and Iran. I have written extensively on each of these countries' nuclear programs and policies. Over the past ten years I also have analyzed nuclear dynamics in Northeast Asia, particularly Chinese and Japanese perspectives on them.

Because time here is short and the range of topics you have asked my colleagues and me to address is extensive, I concentrate my testimony on what I think are some cutting-edge strategic challenges in Northeast Asia and South Asia that need to be more creatively addressed by U.S. policy-makers. These are problems to which no one has tidy, feasible solutions—that is, solutions that would change to our complete satisfaction the military capabilities and behaviors we want other states to change, and thereby significantly reduce risks of conflict that could escalate to the use of nuclear weapons. This is largely because the other states involved have different interests and objectives than the U.S. does and will search for ways to pursue them. Knowing that they cannot compete directly and symmetrically with U.S. conventional and strategic forces, these states will often seek to develop and apply asymmetric capabilities and strategies to balance U.S. power. This is especially true of two of the states under consideration—the DPRK and China—whose governments fear the U.S. seeks ultimately to displace them. The challenge, then, for the U.S. and these states is to achieve tolerable stability, avoid escalatory warfare, and establish ways of getting along through political-diplomatic processes backed by balances of power.

I have divided my testimony into five key points that describe the regional dynamics at play and suggest priority policies the U.S. could pursue to mitigate instabilities and risks of nuclear escalation.

1. Complex causal dynamics drive the threat perceptions and nuclear requirements and policies of states in Northeast Asia and South Asia.

This is an analytic and conceptual point that must be recognized if the U.S. and others are to devise policies and deploy capabilities that will improve security and ameliorate instability in these two inter-related regions. Setting North Korea to the side for a moment, it may help to conceptualize the Northeast Asian and South Asian nuclear ''system'' in the form of two strategic triangles that are connected by a common node, which is China. The following diagram represents this idea.

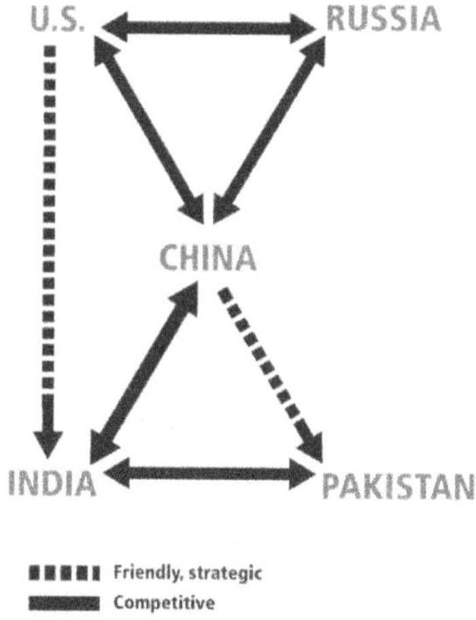

The first triangle includes the U.S., Russia and China. Each of these state's nuclear requirements and policies (as well as non-nuclear instruments of force, deterrence and coercion) affects and is affected by the other two states. For example, the U.S. has long seen Russia as a benchmark for determining U.S. nuclear posture and policy, and recently has factored China more heavily into policy calculations, including regarding strategic conventional weapons, cyberwarfare capabilities, and ballistic missile defenses. China in turn calculates its strategic military requirements and options by reference to current and potential threats that it perceives emanating from the U.S., and to a lesser extent from Russia.

The second triangle includes China, India and Pakistan. India seeks strategic capabilities to deter major aggression from China and from Pakistan today and in the future. Many of the delivery systems and nuclear warhead capabilities India seeks are intended to increase its capacity to deter China, whose current and future capabilities in turn are driven in large part by perceptions of threat from the U.S. Pakistan then seeks nuclear and other capabilities to balance what it perceives India to be acquiring. Many Indian analysts perceive that China is assisting Pakistan's strategic acquisitions, so India seeks not only to balance China, but also to balance the gains Pakistan may achieve in cooperation with China. For its part, Pakistan increasingly perceives the U.S. and India to be cooperating in buttressing Indian military capabilities with which Pakistan must contend.

From the perspective of the United States, the main takeaway from this depiction of the strategic force dynamics involving these states is that policies, capabilities, and operational plans we develop to affect one of these states may cause others also to react in turn.

For example, a former commander of India's strategic forces recently explained to me that "what the U.S. does to extend deterrence to its allies in East Asia affects China which then acts in ways that challenge India. The Chinese note and build up capability, strategy and philosophy to deal with what the U.S. is doing. The Chinese have deployed large numbers of conventionally armed ballistic missiles and cyber capabilities and anti-satellite weapons to deny U.S. forces access into areas sensitive to them, primarily around Taiwan. Those capabilities could be used against India, too."

Pakistanis constantly assert that the so-called U.S.-India nuclear deal could significantly boost India's stockpile of fissile material that could be used to build up its nuclear forces. Similarly, they say, potential U.S. cooperation with India on ballistic missile defenses could require Pakistan to further increase the numbers and diversity of its missile armory and nuclear warhead inventory.

Of course, much the same could be said about China's cooperation with Pakistan and Russia's cooperation with India. This is not to suggest that the U.S. and these other states should desist from all such policies and activities. Rather, the point is that these policies and activities are inter-related more than is commonly recognized. If strategic instability is going to be redressed in Northeast and South Asia, each state, including the U.S. must be more willing than they heretofore have been to acknowledge and address how their own capabilities and actions affect the others. Among other things, this means that prospective policies must be considered in a regional context, not merely a bilateral one.

2. Regarding China, the most fundamental challenge for U.S. policy is to engage Beijing in tempering several forms of security dilemmas and affirming that neither state will initiate the use of force to change the territorial status quo in Northeast and South Asia.

In John Herz's famous words (at least amongst wonks), the security dilemma is "A structural notion in which the self-help attempts of states to look after their security needs tend, regardless of intention, to lead to rising insecurity for others as each interprets its own measures as defensive and measures of others as potentially threatening."

The U.S. and China confront security dilemmas of their own making in at least three domains.

One pertains to concerns of the U.S. and its protectorates—most acutely Taiwan and Japan—that China may use its growing economic and military power to coerce them in territorial and political disputes. China, for its part, has countervailing concerns that the U.S. and its allies may seek to apply military power to advance their preferred positions vis a vis China, particularly in case of a crisis over the political evolution of Taiwan as it relates to China. (China has a deeper concern that the U.S. seeks to subvert its political order and foster democratization. It is difficult for the U.S. to convince Chinese leaders that while we desire political change in their country we do not intend to use our military capabilities and policies to bring this change about). The famous "three communiques" issued by the U.S. and China between 1979 and August 1982[1] created a modus vivendi on these questions related to Taiwan, but both countries remain wary that it could be fragile. Each side in this security dilemma builds military power, and, in the U.S. case occasionally sells arms to Taiwan. Each also sometimes makes political declarations intended to preserve its defensive positions, but which the other side may interpret as expressions of intent to change the status quo.

A second security dilemma arises from each side's build-up of non-nuclear forces—conventionally-armed ballistic missiles, naval and air forces, ballistic missile defenses, and cyberwarfare capabilities—which each justifies as means to defend against the presumed offensive intentions of the other. This dynamic creates arms race instability, whether of a symmetric or asymmetric nature. For example, China for years has steadily augmented its arsenal of conventionally-armed ballistic missiles and anti-satellite weaponry to offset the United States' superior naval power projection capabilities. The United States' ongoing ballistic missile defense program can be seen as an effort to maintain a long-standing asymmetric advantage in the

[1] The third communique, in August 1982, states in part: "The United States Government attached great importance to its relations with China, and reiterates that it has no intention of infringing on Chinese sovereignty and territorial integrity, or interfering in China's internal affairs, or pursuing a policy of "Two Chinas" or "one China, one Taiwan." The United States Government understands and appreciates the Chinese policy of striving for a peaceful resolution of the Taiwan question as indicated in China's Message to Compatriots in Taiwan issued on Jan. 1, 1979, and the nine-point proposal put forward by China on Sept. 30, 1981.

nuclear domain, and as a way to offset China's build-up of conventionally armed ballistic missiles. Both states, led by the U.S., are developing conventional prompt-strike weapons. Additionally, the U.S. and China both are engaged in a cyberweapon arms race, with China trying to catch up to the U.S.

A third security dilemma exists in the domain of nuclear policy. China fears that the U.S. seeks to acquire means to negate its nuclear deterrent, through some combination of offensive nuclear forces, future hypersonic conventionally-armed missiles, ballistic missile defenses, and cyberwarfare capabilities.

China is assessed to possess approximately 250 nuclear warheads. It is assessed to deploy between 50–75 ballistic missiles capable of carrying nuclear weapons to the United States, and another approximately 60 intermediate range ballistic missiles suited for use against India, Japan or Taiwan. By comparison the United States' operationally deploys 2,200 nuclear weapons. China is estimated to possess an additional 16 tonnes of highly-enriched uranium and 1.8 tonnes of non-civilian separated plutonium, compared to the United States' stockpile of 604 tonnes and 87 tonnes, respectively. The U.S. and its protégés fear that China may someday add dramatically to its nuclear forces in ways that would undermine—along with conventional anti-access area-denial capabilities—the American deterrent extended to Taiwan and Japan. Each side in this competition does not adequately acknowledge how its own actions drive the other to take the actions that it sees as threatening.

To deal with these challenges, the U.S. does not need more or different nuclear forces than it already possesses and plans to possess after implementation of the New Start Treaty with Russia. In terms of capabilities, the greater imperative is to acquire and/or deploy non-nuclear instruments to preserve the United States' capacity to quickly defend its protectorates against and to deter Chinese actions to initiate changes in the territorial status quo in the region. Such potential Chinese actions are very unlikely to involve its nuclear forces, and it is thus in the U.S. interest to counter with strong, symmetrical conventional capabilities.

A more immediately pressing need is to motivate Chinese leaders to join the U.S. and, where appropriate its allies, in articulating and authenticating policies that would reassure all sides in these security dilemmas that they will not initiate the use of force to change the territorial or political status quo or to otherwise coerce each other. To this end, it will be necessary for Chinese officials to understand the concept of the security dilemma and recognize how their words and deeds sometimes exacerbate it.

With regard to nuclear policy, the key dilemma concerns first-use of nuclear weapons. Retaliatory use of nuclear weapons is a comparatively straightforward proposition; the destabilizing factor is the prospect that the U.S. or China would initiate attacks—by nuclear, conventional, or cyber means—on the other's nuclear deterrent forces and/or their command and control systems. The U.S. would be wise to overcome its politically motivated reluctance to assure China that it will not seek to negate China's nuclear deterrent. Washington should do this out of recognition that mutual nuclear vulnerability is a fact of 21st century life with China, and attempting to negate this fact through a combination of new offensive and defensive systems would not succeed at a cost that the U.S. would find acceptable to itself. The language authored by a 2009 Council on Relations Task Force on U.S. Nuclear Policy chaired by William Perry and Brent Scowcroft could be a model: "mutual vulnerability with China—like mutual vulnerability with Russia—is not a policy choice to be embraced or rejected, but rather a strategic fact to be managed with priority on strategic stability."

For its part, China should be motivated to reciprocate constructively by clarifying that as long as U.S. policies and military capabilities reflect this assurance China will not significantly increase its nuclear weapon arsenal and threaten to use force to alter the territorial status quo and/or resolve "the Taiwan question."

Such declarations of fundamental policy would not preclude the U.S., China, or other states from modernizing and bolstering their strategic offensive and defensive capabilities, but they would provide a framework within which each party could explain to the other how its actions are not inconsistent with fundamentally defensive intentions and assurances. This would be constructive on its own terms, and could eventually create conditions for possible negotiation of arms limitations.

3. One of the most complicated challenges facing U.S. policy-makers today is to reassure Japan that the U.S. has the resolve and capabilities to defend it against armed attack from China or any other state.

Extended deterrence is never easy to provide or depend upon. The protégé often will fear that its protector will abandon it. At other times, the protégé may fear that the protector will entrap it in a war that the protégé would otherwise seek to avoid. The guarantor, on the other hand, must convince the protégé as well as the adversary that the guarantor will put its soldiers and citizens and treasury at risk in order to defend another. This is especially problematic insofar as the protégé may itself act in ways that instigate a potential conflict, raising legitimate questions about whether the guarantor should or would invite the costs of coming to its defense in such a situation.

Extended deterrence is often conflated with extended nuclear deterrence. While it may be tempting to believe that the potential use of nuclear weapons always strengthens extended deterrence, the issue is problematic. Potential use of nuclear weapons in an escalating conflict can indeed strengthen the potency of the guarantor's deterrent against a potential aggressor. But the very destructiveness that this portends also can weaken the resolve of the guarantor state's population (should we trade Los Angeles for Taipei?) as well as the protégé's population (if the U.S. uses nuclear weapons on China, China will respond first by targeting nuclear weapons at Japan). These possible reactions may tempt a potential aggressor into thinking that the mere threat of aggression that could escalate to nuclear use can split an alliance, or demonstrate the guarantor's weak resolve, constituting a bluff that may be called.

On the other hand, if the guarantor's resolve is unquestioned in the face of a countervailing nuclear threat, nuclear moral hazards may be created. Like a finance company whose managers believe that the government will bail them out if they face ruinous losses, the protégé may take unwise risks in its policies toward its adversary, feeling that the nuclear threat proffered by the guarantor will deter the adversary from reacting forcefully. The protégé also may under-invest in non-nuclear defensive capabilities that would otherwise obviate the need to resort to nuclear threats to deter the adversary, like a bank that does not maintain conservative levels of reserves to cover its commitments.

This sort of hazard has long affected the United States' relations with its NATO allies, most of whom do not meet their commitments to devote two percent of their GDP to defense. Japan, too, has not always carried its full share of the defense burden with the United States. Its defense spending declined between 2002 and the arrival of the new Abe government in 2013. Now Japan is pursuing plans for an increase in procurement of major systems, and the U.S. and Japan have intensified exercises and other cooperative activities to solidify defense in the East China Sea. Still, the national government in Tokyo has not successfully overcome local governments' reluctance to cooperate in relocating U.S. military bases on Okinawa. It is common in Washington to hear complaints that an administration is not doing enough to reassure Japan of the United States' commitment to defend it; it is less common to hear of even private congressional remonstrances to Japanese officials that they should do more to buttress the alliance materially and diplomatically (vis a vis Japan's neighbors). A careful complementarity is required to match increases in defense preparedness with political and diplomatic sensitivity to the concerns this can cause in states that experienced Japanese aggression in the 1930s.

These considerations can be applied to the issue that currently poses the greatest risk of potential conflict involving Japan and China, and implicating the U.S. as Japan's protector. There is a cluster of islands and rock outcroppings in the East China Sea that Japan calls the Senkaku Islands and China calls the Diaoyu Islands. Japan incorporated the islands under the administration of Okinawa, in January 1895, during the first Sino-Japanese War. The U.S. took control of these outcroppings as a result of World War II, and returned them to Japanese control in 1972. China disputes Japan's right to sovereignty over these islands. The U.S. does not offer a judgment on the disputed claims to sovereignty, but says that the islands fall within the territory the U.S. is obligated by treaty to help Japan defend. The Japanese government in late 2012 bought the islands from a private owner, explaining that it did so to prevent the nationalist governor of Tokyo from acquiring and developing them. Reflecting the logic of security dilemmas, China intensified its contestation over the issue, and deployed naval vessels and aircraft around and over the islands in order to manifest its claim and pressure Japan to proceed carefully. A non-trivial risk now appears that either state could act physically to change the status quo on or around these islands, and/or that the naval vessels or aircraft could collide, as happened with a Chinese fishing vessel and a Japanese Coast Guard ship in 2010. Such collisions could create a severe crisis that the highly nationalistic Chinese and Japanese governments could find difficult to de-escalate.

Were such a crisis to occur when China and Japan are led by strength-projecting nationalistic figures, the U.S. would face excruciatingly complex challenges. The first priority would be to resolve the crisis diplomatically. But this could be very difficult to do, depending on the circumstances. Japan and China would dispute whose actors and actions were to blame for the precipitating action. If the U.S. did not take its ally Japan's side, whatever the merits of the case, some faction in Washington would decry the abandonment of an ally. If Japan were at fault and the U.S. did not acknowledge this for political-diplomatic reasons, China would become even more determined to press its claims on this dispute and others that involve U.S. allies. If evidence held that China was at fault, the political-diplomatic position of the U.S. would be simpler, but then the U.S. and Japan would likely find themselves in a potentially escalating conflict with China.

In either case, to augment diplomacy and strengthen deterrence, and to prevail in case diplomacy fails, the U.S. and Japan would need to have the conventional military means to prevent China from creating new ''facts on the ground,'' for example by physically taking control of the islands. Failure to ensure this initial defense could create a situation where the U.S. and Japan would feel compelled to fight China to reverse its gain. Such a conflict could escalate and expand to a wider naval battle or blockade contest as each leadership would feel its credibility and political survival at stake. Were the U.S. and Japan not prevailing, someone in Washington or Tokyo would at least raise the prospect that the conflict could escalate to the use of nuclear weapons. After all, that's how nuclear deterrence is supposed to work. Yet, would even implying a nuclear threat be advisable and therefore credible? Would and should the United States be willing to risk nuclear war over uninhabited rocks in East Asia that 99 percent of the American people have never heard of and could not find on a map? Recall, the issue here would be first-use of nuclear weapons: if China, despite its commitment and force posture of no-first-use, took steps signaling that it would break the nuclear taboo, U.S. recourse to retaliatory nuclear weapons reasonably would be on the table. But threatening to initiate the use of nuclear weapons in conflict that erupted over these disputed outcroppings—no matter how far it escalated—would constitute a profound over-reaction.

Japanese leaders and citizens may not appreciate this analysis. They may prefer to over-rely on the magic of nuclear deterrence. But statesmanship requires realism, dealing with facts and assessing strategic risks. Japan and the United States must recognize the imperative of developing and deploying diplomacy and conventional military power to prevent efforts by anyone to forcibly change the status quo surrounding this territorial dispute. The combination of clear commitments not to upset the status quo and demonstrable non-nuclear means to prevent anyone else from physically changing it constitutes the strongest possible extended deterrent, for it reaffirms a fundamentally defensive posture that augments national and international resolve.

The current and projected nuclear arsenal of the United States is more than sufficient to perform the physical requirements of extending nuclear deterrence to Japan against China. Nor is it evident that ''strengthening'' U.S. declaratory policy regarding the use of nuclear weapons would enhance (and not otherwise undermine) the feasibility and durability of the extended nuclear deterrent.

4. North Korea will not in the foreseeable future agree to relinquish all of its nuclear weapons and related capabilities. The near-term imperative should be to negotiate constraints on the buildup of DPRK nuclear capabilities and enforceable commitments not to transfer them to others.

Japanese and South Korean leaders are politically and psychologically unprepared to negotiate anything less than complete DPRK disarmament, for complex reasons. This in turn intensifies political pressures on any American administration not to deviate from this stated objective. This motivates North Korea to demand an exorbitant price for cooperation, which its interlocutors doubt the DPRK will fully implement in any case.

A more realistic alternative would be to bargain for incremental steps by the DPRK to stop increasing its nuclear stockpile and to eschew proliferation of nuclear materials and know-how to other actors. These forms of restraint by the DPRK could be more achievable at a lower price than the DPRK seeks for the illusory objective of total nuclear disarmament.

Acknowledging that DPRK will retain some nuclear weapons for the foreseeable future offends our sense of virtue, as does embarking on what amounts to a protection-racket arrangement to pay the DPRK for not damaging the neighborhood. But the perfect may be the enemy of the somewhat tolerable here: by acknowledging that the DPRK would retain a limited nuclear capability to satisfy its regime's need to deter U.S. and other efforts to displace it, the U.S. and other negotiating parties would strengthen their leverage to obtain North Korean cooperation in mitigating its other threatening behaviors. Arguably, this is the best outcome that might be achieved today.

For such an adjustment in negotiating objectives to be sustainable, the U.S., Japan, South Korea, China and Russia would need to devise a formula that would affirm their ultimate goal to be the creation of a regional security environment free of nuclear weapons on the Korean Peninsula. Such a goal is necessary to satisfy the political-psychological needs of South Korea and Japan. Yet, the prospect of freeing the Korean Peninsula of all nuclear weapons and (still to be defined) supporting infrastructure would be more realistic after the relevant parties had incrementally built mutual confidence by stopping the expansion of North Korea's nuclear arsenal and infrastructure and authenticating that the DPRK was not transferring weapons, material, and know-how to others.

In terms of U.S. nuclear force requirements and posture, the nuclear threat posed by the DPRK is a lesser-included challenge that can be more than adequately covered by nuclear (and non-nuclear) forces that the U.S. will retain as part of its larger requirement to deter Russia and China.

5. India and Pakistan will continue to augment their nuclear arsenals. The imperatives now are to prevent another major terrorist attack from Pakistan against India and reduce the risks of escalation to nuclear war.

South Asia is the most likely place nuclear weapons could be detonated in the foreseeable future. This risk derives from the unusual dynamic of the India-Pakistan competition. The next major terrorist attack in India, emanating from Pakistan, may trigger an Indian conventional military riposte that could in turn prompt Pakistan to use battlefield nuclear weapons to repel an Indian incursion. India, for its part, has declared that it would inflict massive retaliation in response to any nuclear use against its territory or troops. Obviously, this threatening dynamic—whereby terrorism may prompt conventional conflict which may prompt nuclear war—challenges Indian and Pakistan policy-makers. India and Pakistan both tend to downplay or dismiss the potential for escalation, but our own history of close nuclear calls should make U.S. officials more alert to these dangers. The U.S. is the only outside power that could intervene diplomatically and forcefully to de-escalate a crisis.

India, is believed to possess approximately 90–110 nuclear weapons. It plans to deliver them via aircraft and/or a growing fleet of ballistic and perhaps cruise missiles. Available information suggests it keeps the nuclear bombs and warheads separate from their aircraft and missile delivery systems. With a historically entrenched doctrine of No First Use, and a strict insistence on civilian control over nuclear policy, India plans to mate weapons and delivery systems only when the need for their potential use appears imminent. While India retains significant quantities of plutonium outside of civilian control, which it conceivably could use to dramatically expand its nuclear arsenal, India thus far rejects ideas of nuclear war-fighting and corresponding development of a large nuclear arsenal, much as China does.

Pakistan is estimated to have 100–120 nuclear weapons, with a continually growing capacity to produce plutonium and highly-enriched uranium to expand this arsenal if it chooses to. Pakistan continues to add new missile delivery capabilities to its arsenal. Most noteworthy has been the development of the NASR 60-kilometre range missile, which Pakistan projects as a battlefield weapon to deter Indian ground-force incursions into its territory. Pakistan proffers the threat of initiating nuclear use if and when it would be necessary to defeat what it would perceive as Indian aggression from land, air and/or sea.

India faces two inter-related strategic challenges vis a vis Pakistan: to compel Pakistani authorities to curtail the operations of anti-Indian terrorists; and to deter Pakistan from engaging in escalatory warfare if and when India responds violently to a terrorist attack. The new prime minister of India, Narendra Modi came to power with a reputation for strong action, which he and his supporters juxtapose to the perceived weakness of his predecessors. Indeed, Modi's government recently unleashed the Indian Army to retaliate with disproportionate force against traditional Pakistani artillery shelling across the disputed Line of Control in Kashmir. Senior advisors to the prime minister have said that there should be little doubt he will respond forcefully if India is attacked again by terrorists associated with Pakistan.

The questions are, what strategy (or strategies) and capabilities would be feasible and effective to enable India to motivate Pakistan's security establishment to demobilize anti-India terrorist groups? If terrorist attacks cannot be prevented, how can India respond to them in ways that minimize risks of escalation that would be unfavorable to India?

Since the major Indo-Pak crisis of 2001–2002 following a terrorist attack on India's parliament building, Indians have debated options ranging from Army-centric ground thrusts into Pakistan, precision air strikes, covert operations, and non-kinetic efforts to isolate and sanction Pakistan.

Clearly, some actions that could most probably satisfy one of India's multiple domestic and bilateral objectives would lessen the chances of achieving others. For example, satisfying the desire to punish Pakistan could be achieved by a relatively wide range of military actions and international economic sanctions. But the more destructive of possible military actions could raise the overall scale and costs of the conflict to levels disproportionate to the harm done by the initial attack on India, and invite unwelcome international responses. For example, a successful ground campaign into Pakistan would be most likely to prompt Pakistan to use battlefield nuclear weapons to stop Indian forces and compel them to leave Pakistani territory.

No theories in the existing international literature or in other states' practices offer guidance regarding how India could most effectively proceed here. Studies of strategies and tactics to deter and defeat terrorism have not addressed situations when the major antagonists possess nuclear weapons. Theories and case studies of nuclear deterrence and escalation management in a nuclearized environment have not involved cases where terrorists with unclear relationships to one of the state antagonists are the instigators of aggression and the "unitary rational actor" model may not apply. The Indo-Pak competition features both sets of challenges with the added complication that third states—primarily the U.S. and China—also figure heavily in the calculations of decision-makers.

All of this has implications for U.S. policy-makers. Historically and today, the U.S. has not planned for its nuclear forces to serve deterring or war-fighting roles against Pakistan and/or India. Thus, South Asian scenarios do not figure in calculating the adequacy of U.S. nuclear forces.

However, there are possible scenarios in which the U.S. could become directly implicated in nuclear crises with Pakistan and/or between India and Pakistan. Pakistan fears that the U.S. in certain circumstances might conduct military operations to capture or otherwise neutralize Pakistan's nuclear forces and fissile materials. Indeed, one of the most telling Pakistani reactions to the U.S. raid that killed Osama Bin Laden was to intensify efforts to hide and secure their nuclear assets. Some of these protective steps could be welcome insofar as they also could help secure Pakistan's nuclear assets against possible efforts by militant non-state actors or rebelling military units to capture them. This scenario—radicals in Pakistan acquiring nuclear weapons and/or fissile materials—has alarmed successive U.S. administrations. Given fears of nuclear terrorism, it would be reasonable for relevant U.S. government actors to aspire to have the precise intelligence and capabilities required to, in a crisis, locate Pakistan's nuclear assets and seek to remove or disable them. Whether the U.S. has the requisite capabilities cannot be gleaned from public sources, but the task would be extremely daunting given the number of Pakistan's nuclear weapons, the volume of its fissile material, and their dispersal to well-hidden and defended facilities.

In any case, while some Pakistani authorities might welcome a successful U.S. operation during an internal Pakistani crisis to keep the country's nuclear weapon capabilities from falling into the hands of anti-state groups, the possibility of such an operation would generally be seen as deeply threatening to Pakistan. Few would be confident that the U.S. would only intervene when it might be welcomed; all would worry that the U.S. might intervene in a very different scenario in which Pakistan was embroiled in a conflict with India. Indeed, the worst nightmare for Pakistani strategic planners is a combined U.S.-Indian effort to negate, or at least degrade, their nuclear deterrent.

This may seem far-fetched today, and I am unaware of scholarly or official analyses of such a possibility. However, I think the following questions suggest that it would behoove the U.S. government to work discreetly on this problem. If India and Pakistan become embroiled in a major military conflict following a major terrorist attack on India attributed to Pakistan, and the U.S. detects Pakistan to be readying nuclear forces for use, should the U.S. intervene to prevent the use of nuclear weapons?

Consider that the U.S. and India are now self-proclaimed strategic partners, and many thousands of Americans live in India or regularly visit it, reflecting ever-increasing U.S. commercial investments and interests in India. Consider also the large and prominent Indian-American community who feel passionately about their native home and participate ever more actively in American politics. If nuclear weapons were being readied for use, with a real prospect of escalation to nuclear war between India and Pakistan, would U.S. leaders feel they should simply stand back and watch? If, God forbid, nuclear weapons were detonated and Americans were among the casualties, would not Congress demand an inquiry to learn "what did the president know and when did he know it, and why did he or she not act to try to prevent it?" Would there not be an expectation that the government had done contingency planning for such an emergency, given how long Pakistan and India have had nuclear weapons and how central the U.S. has been in resolving earlier crises between them?

Members of Congress are much better positioned to answer these questions than I am. But I would wager that there is some prospect that U.S. leaders would at least be expected to have prepared for such a contingency, even if the preparations concluded there was little that could be done physically to prevent it.

Indeed, we should assume that Pakistani military strategists are thinking of scenarios in which the U.S. might alone, or in cooperation with India, intervene in a looming nuclear conflict to stay Pakistan's hand. In this case, Pakistani planners will be considering whether and how they could deter the U.S. from such intervention. Of course, inviting war, possibly nuclear war, with the United States would be a terrible risk. But in a scenario in which Pakistani military leaders were considering nuclear war with India already, and the U.S. was seen to be denying this recourse to a perceived existential necessity, this could be a risk that they could be willing to threaten to run.

I close by suggesting that, as in the earlier discussion concerning Northeast Asia, the nuclear challenges in South Asia will not be redressed by more or newer U.S. nuclear weapons or changes in U.S. nuclear doctrine. There is no evidence to the contrary. The most immediately pressing objective of U.S. policy should be to apply vigorous, creative diplomatic and political energy to prevent another crisis between India and Pakistan, and if one cannot be prevented, to enhance the preparation of Indian, Pakistani and American officials to manage it with minimal escalation.

Senator SESSIONS. Well, those are thoughtful and great issues to discuss. Thank you for sharing your thoughts and leadership with us.

Dr. Krepinevich, Henry Kissinger testified a few weeks ago before the Armed Services Committee, and he was pretty animated—and it is in his book, too—about what he considers an alteration of our initial negotiating policy with Iran, to accept them getting within months of having a nuclear weapon. He expressed the concern at the hearing that this creates a circumstance where Turkey, Saudi, Egypt may feel if they are within months of weapon, then they practically have one, and they need to have one.

What thoughts would you have about that danger and what we can do to prevent it?

Dr. KREPINEVICH. Well, certainly if I were a neighbor of Iran's, and we are looking at a short sprint to a nuclear weapon, if the declared goal now is to keep them a year out, that assumes, I believe the Deputy Secretary of State said, an unprecedented level of intrusion and verification to keep them at that level. The question is, can we achieve that?

So far, I think the history has been that the cheaters often seem to have an advantage. Even President Reagan, who was famous for saying "trust but verify," during his presidency, the Soviets were cheating on the ABM Treaty and on the biological conventions treaty.

Our success in trying to impose constraints on countries like North Korea and Iran has been limited at best and unfortunate at worst. So I think it would be very difficult, as I said in my testimony, absent a clear threat of military action or military action, to get the Iranians, at this point, given the investment they have made, the trouble they have gone through, the damage to their reputation they have sustained, to deflect them.

You can see that there are clear benefits to Iran from having a nuclear capability, both in terms of regime preservation, which I assume is probably their top priority, and then advancing their aims throughout the region.

Senator SESSIONS. Well, I think, so if you are a Saudi Arabian, and you think you have the ability to achieve a nuclear weapon through research or money, then if you think your adversary is within months, 12, 9, I believe—actually, I think Kissinger used the word ''9 months,'' then you could have a proliferation.

How dangerous would it be if we ended up with Turkey, Saudi Arabia, and Egypt with nuclear weapons?

Dr. KREPINEVICH. Well, I would say it is certainly——

Senator SESSIONS. Anything that our nuclear arsenal should be altered to deal with that?

Dr. KREPINEVICH. Under those circumstance where, say, you had a nuclear-armed Saudi Arabia next to Iran, as I mentioned earlier, the ability to have an effective attack warning system and command and control system would certainly test the limits of technology, test the resources of both countries, both in terms of financial and in terms of the manpower resources.

During the Cold War when we were placing the Pershing 2s into Western Europe, the Soviets at the time, according to the documentation that has come out, actually explored an option called the ''dead hand,'' which is—if you have seen the movie ''Dr. Strangelove,'' it is an automated nuclear response mechanism, because they were concerned that the Pershings would give them such little warning time that they might be faced with a decapitation attack. They eventually moved toward something I understand called ''perimeter,'' which is semi-automated.

In this case, I think what we might be able to offer countries like Saudi Arabia, hopefully, is, to the extent that we can, effective attack warning. Perhaps a willingness, hopefully, to dissuade them from acquiring their own nuclear weapons by offering extended deterrence. The possibility of missile defense, although I am skeptical about missile defense for a couple of reasons.

One is in the Cold War, we had nuclear plenty before we had missile plenty, and we went to MIRV systems. So the problem we faced right now is opposite, in the sense that Iran has missile plenty, but not nuclear plenty.

So in a short-range attack on Saudi Arabia, if they did not need—if they could go beyond the Shahab-3 missiles and use some 1s and 2s, they may create a problem for us in terms of having a lot of decoys—maybe 4 or 5 missiles with nuclear warheads on it, 20 or 30 missiles in the attack overall, and force our missile defenses to actually engage them all. We would be at the losing end of a missile defense proposition.

Senator SESSIONS. You do think providing a nuclear umbrella to our allies in the region is something that would have to be considered?

Dr. KREPINEVICH. Certainly, I think so. Again, this is—I think there is a lot of virgin strategic territory here.

Senator SESSIONS. Would we then need to move advance locations for our nuclear weapons, if that were to occur?

Dr. KREPINEVICH. Again, I would want to think through the issue. I was about to say that if you had, as you said, multiple states—Turkey, Saudi Arabia, Iran—and just for a thought experiment, each had 50 nuclear weapons, then if you are the Saudis, you may have to plan against an attack by 100 nuclear weapons. You cannot have parity with everyone in an end-state competition.

To the extent the United States provides nuclear guarantees, that could offset some of the fears that, in fact, even though I am inferior numerically in terms of nuclear weapons, the United States can help make up the difference.

So, again, we have never really, to my knowledge, gotten into a detailed analysis of end-state nuclear competitions, especially when warning times are extremely short, and as George points out, you are looking at other factors, such as the ability of conventional weapons to substitute for nuclear weapons, advanced defenses, cyber weaponry, and so on.

Senator SESSIONS. Well, it is definitely a complex thing. It seems to me that if you have got now Iran, Saudi Arabia, other nations with nuclear weapons, you have got four Nations perhaps who would use nuclear weapons if their existence is at threat. So you have increased danger of a first use in the ways that we maybe have not thought through.

Dr. KREPINEVICH. Certainly, you have more triggers—fingers on the trigger. I would be interested in my colleagues' reaction, too.

One thing, of course, that concerns some folks is the Saudi-Pakistani connection. Should Pakistan, for example, deploy weapons in Saudi Arabia, certain countries—Israel included—might view that as weapons, even though they are under nominal Pakistani control, actually being under the de facto control of the Saudis. While, at the same time, what is the view of India? Does India view this move as an effort by Pakistan to create strategic depth in terms of its nuclear forces?

So I think George was getting to this point. You cannot just segment these particular problems by region. In some cases, they are transregionalproblems.

Senator SESSIONS. Thank you. These are so complex, but I think we better give up my time to Senator Donnelly. I have hogged too many minutes.

Senator DONNELLY. Thank you, Mr. Chairman.

Dr. Perkovich, you know we have spoken to General Campbell recently, and he talked about how relations between he and the Pakistan army are better than they have been in a very, very, very long time. Then you flip to the nuclear side, and you have Pakistan increasingly perceiving the United States and India to be cooperating together, and it puts them in a tougher spot, Pakistan feels.

How do you balance off this?

Dr. PERKOVICH. It is a great question, and you might get a good debate going with Ashley and me, but I do not——

Senator DONNELLY. On the one side, we are supposedly working better than ever, and it is like going down the hall into another room, and you have a completely 180 perspective.

Dr. PERKOVICH. I think I work back from—and this does not go over really well in Pakistan, but sometimes, you know, you just stick with something if you believe it is true.

Senator DONNELLY. We just want to know what you think.

Dr. PERKOVICH. The good news is India has no desires for any Pakistani territory or anything in Pakistan. So, the "threat from India" is only in response to Pakistani aggression in India, or terrorism in India.

That is a basis for the United States in our relations with the Pakistanis to say, look, if we can cooperate in getting at the terrorism problem within Pakistan, what you are worried about from

India goes away, number one. Number two, the influence that we might have in India can help reassure you of that, which, by the way, did happen in 2001 and 2002. Ashley was out in Delhi in the embassy there—there was a crisis—where the U.S. was trying to stay both of their hands.

So there is a basis, if you can get at the terrorism problem. If Pakistan cannot commit itself to working against the terrorists that have operated in India, then there is not much we can do to reassure them, but I would argue there is probably not much we should do to reassure them because that really is a problem.

Senator DONNELLY. Let me ask you—and this is not exactly on the nuclear topic, but do you see it as a long-term gamechanger what happened with the Army Public School in Pakistan recently, to their children, when the attack took place?

Do you see them having like a long-term commitment to eliminating the Taliban, or is that something that you think 6 months, a year from now may fade away?

Dr. Tellis?

Dr. TELLIS. It is a difficult question to answer at this point, but what we have certainly seen is that the Pakistan army seems to be much more energized about going after terrorist groups that are wrecking havoc within Pakistani society. I think that is welcome, and of course, it has been long overdue.

The question that cannot be answered today is whether the Pakistanis will now extend this effort to groups that do not directly threaten Pakistan but threaten others—groups that threaten Afghanistan, United States forces in Afghanistan, and India. Thus far, we have seen a very energetic Pakistani response to their own state enemies. All things being equal, we would want to see that rather than the absence.

But I think we would declare victory only when Pakistanis begin to think of terrorism in a sort of broader context and begin to focus their attentions on all terrorist groups, and not pick and choose between groups that support their interests and groups that support them.

Senator DONNELLY. How strong are their security efforts around their nuclear weapons? How good are their programs and processes, as you have seen, compared to other nations?

Dr. PERKOVICH. On this one, I could say nuclear weapons are the most secure thing in Pakistan. That is good news and bad news.

Senator DONNELLY. Well, I am the tallest person in my family.

Dr. PERKOVICH. I am the shortest in mine.

Senator DONNELLY. Everything is degree.

Dr. PERKOVICH. But the issue is, is that—that is not the problem I would focus on precisely because it is one that they care about more than anything, the army. They have capabilities, and capabilities are acquirable to deal with that. So they may not be perfect at it, but they are on the job, and there is a reason to think they can manage it.

The problem that is much harder is, again, the terrorism leads to the war, which leads to escalation. So it is not the loss of nuclear weapons, it is actually the use of nuclear weapons in a conflict to me is a more probable scenario. It has implications for us that are not as dire as a nuclear terrorist attack on the United States, but that are pretty dire when you start going through the calculation. So that is the unattended-to problem that I think we need to focus on.

Senator DONNELLY. Thank you, Doctor.

Thank you, Mr. Chairman.

Senator SESSIONS. Senator Fischer?

Senator FISCHER. Thank you, Mr. Chairman.

I would like to open this up for any of you if you would like to make a comment on it.

I would like to know what influence we have as a country if we see the confidence of our allies being eroded over what they would view as the protection of a nuclear umbrella that we would have in the region.

Also what influence we would have over trying to prevent proliferation amongst our allies in different regions, when we see conflicts continuing to grow, and the ability of our allies to acquire nuclear capabilities, either on developing them on their own or being able to purchase them elsewhere.

If I will open that up.

Dr. KROENIG. Well, it is an important question, and I think our extended deterrent depends in part on our capability. Do we have the capability to follow through? It also depends on the credibility. Will we do it?

So going back to the question that was asked of Dr. Krepinevich on Iran, I think that is one of the things that would make deterring a nuclear-armed Iran very difficult and would make reassuring our allies in the region very difficult, would be the lack of United States credibility in that situation. After three successive United States presidents said a nuclear-armed Iran is unacceptable, Iran will not acquire nuclear weapons, and in the end, we allow them to acquire nuclear weapons.

A deterrence and containment regime would rest on U.S. threats. It would rest on U.S. threats to use nuclear weapons, if necessary, to stop Iran, to go to war with a nuclear-armed Iran. So who would believe that we would be prepared to go to war with a nuclear-armed Iran if we were not prepared to go to war with a non-nuclear Iran?

Also, capability is important. So when we think about Asia, and in Dr. Perkovich's testimony he said that China has a secure second-strike capability. We are vulnerable to China, whether we like it or not, and I think that is true. But we need to think about reassuring the allies in the region as well, and something that the allies say is that they would be very uncomfortable with nuclear parity between the United States and China.

So I think one way to square the circle is to make sure, even if China has a secure second-strike capability, to make sure that we maintain nuclear superiority over China. I think that would be one way that China could feel secure that it is not going to be vulnerable to a nuclear strike, but also our allies in the region would feel confident under the American nuclear umbrella.

Senator FISCHER. Thank you. Yes?

Dr. PERKOVICH. I will add a little to this.

A big part of the—as Matt said—of the reassurance, which goes to the heart of your question, Senator, you know, is our resolve.

This is something that you all would have to address, and it is a political issue. How much do you think the American people should be willing to sacrifice to defend Saudi Arabia? How would you sell that politically?

Most of the terrorists that we have dealt with have an ideology that was propagated by Saudi Arabia, often in facilities funded by Saudis. The human rights record in Saudi Arabia is whatever it is. I remember the House years ago would not let the UAE [United Arab Emirates] buy a port facility in—now we are going to talk about extending security guarantees?

So it is a political issue that is first and foremost. They do not doubt our military capabilities. They see what we can do with conventional. They saw what we did in Iraq, 3 weeks gone. The issue is political, and do they think that the United States would actually defend them to the hilt, life or death, is a political issue, much more than it is a hardware issue.

Senator FISCHER. But do you not think it ties into a hardware issue when we know we need to modernize our arsenal, and we are not stepping forward and providing the resources necessary to do even that?

You know, it was said earlier that we are increasing America's commitments and decreasing America's capabilities. That was, in my opinion, a statement that hit the nail on the head. That is where the focus, I think, needs to be for us to be able to move forward with any kind of credibility in this world.

Dr. PERKOVICH. Absolutely. You absolutely have to modernize it, and everything else.

But if you are talking about, for example, in the Middle East, an Iran with 1 weapon—or 10 weapons or 20 weapons—whatever scenario you have about the United States force, which is at 2,200 now, it is probably going to be adequate as long as it is modernized, it is up to date. No one is questioning that.

Senator FISCHER. But as we continue to make commitments around the world, though?

Dr. TELLIS. Can I take a crack at that?

I think the point you are making is a very important one, and particularly in East Asia. The best anti-proliferation measure we have is the robustness of our nuclear umbrella. To the degree that the allies feel reassured by the resilience and the strength of the nuclear umbrella, their incentives to go the nuclear route independently are diminished.

Now, we have been blessed with allies, at least in East Asia, which are advanced industrial societies. If they choose to go the nuclear route, they could go there very, very quickly. So it becomes extremely important for us to be able to maintain our nuclear assets in good repair so that we do not have to incur the temptation—or they do not have to incur the temptation of going there.

Having said that, however, to my mind, when one thinks about this strategically, the real challenge actually is for us to beef up our conventional capabilities, so that if they ever get into a fistfight with some adversaries, we have the capacity to defend them conventionally, such that we do not press too strongly on our nuclear assets.

Let me put it this way. If you get into a fistfight in East Asia, I would rather be in a position where we are so good and so robust conventionally that the other guy has to think about using nuclear weapons first. If somebody else has to start thinking about using nuclear weapons first, then I have the nuclear Reserves necessary to deter them.

If I end up being in a position where I have to use nuclear weapons first because my conventional capabilities are essentially less than robust, then I end up in a very, very uncomfortable and unfavorable world. That is the world we want to avoid.

So we have to do two things simultaneously. You have to make certain that the big stick that is essentially our U.S. strategic Reserves are kept in good shape. But it is our usable forces that we will employ in the course of any conventional problem that really have to be beefed up so that we never have to use our own nuclear weapons if we are forced to.

Senator FISCHER. Thank you.

Thank you, Mr. Chairman.

Senator SESSIONS. Senator King?

Senator KING. You guys are full of good news.

[Laughter.]

Dr. Kroenig, I have never heard anybody deliver such appalling information so calmly before. The sentence that I seized on that you said in your testimony was, "The ongoing conflict in the Ukraine is very much a nuclear crisis."

That is a very important piece of information. I have been to probably a dozen hearings in the last couple of months where the issue of arming the Ukraine has come up, and for a while, at least 2 or 3 weeks ago, it was sort of the wise guy consensus. Oh, yes, this is what we have to do.

I sense there is a bit of a pause, but my question is do you see a danger of escalation, a risk of miscalculation? Given Russia's historic paranoia about the West, all those factors, give me your thoughts on arming the Ukrainians and danger of escalation.

Dr. KROENIG. Well, I think this feeds in a little bit to the point that Dr. Tellis was just making, where if you can deter an adversary at the conventional level or defeat the adversary at the conventional level, you may be able to prevent the conflict from escalating up to the nuclear level. So I am less concerned about Ukraine, in part because the United States does not have as great a stake in Ukraine.

What I worry about a little bit more is if President Putin were to kind of re-run this playbook against a NATO ally, against a Baltic State. Those—if they are NATO allies, we would be compelled to come to their defense. In those kind of situations, if President Putin were making these same kind of nuclear threats, I think the stakes would be much higher because it is a NATO ally, and I think there is a much greater risk for escalation in that kind of scenario.

Senator KING. I understand that. A point well taken.

I guess to get back to Ukraine, though, my concern is that we do not live in a static universe, and we cannot assume that our escalation is the end of the story. To me it appears, as an outsider, that this is of more vital interest to the Russians than it is to us.

Whatever we do, they can match and raise us. That, I said in a hearing the other day, if you are playing chess with a Russian, you better think at least three moves ahead.

Changing the subject briefly. The danger of a terrorist group getting a nuclear weapon somehow—buying, stealing, whatever. Our whole theory of nuclear deterrence over the past 70 years has rested upon a premise of state actors who are somewhat rational and fear death.

What is our strategy to deal with people who are not state actors and want to die? Anybody?

Dr. PERKOVICH. It has to be prevention. The stuff we are doing and probably can always do well.

I mean, the good news on the nuclear piece of terrorism is to actually get a device that will go boom in a very big way requires highly enriched uranium or plutonium, which exists in finite quantities in knowable locations. So it is a problem that governments can actually redress with some degree of confidence. It is not like ending poverty or a lot of other things that one might want.

Senator KING. It is a technical challenge.

Dr. PERKOVICH. It is a technical challenge and a political will challenge. I mean, and this administration has—especially with all the nuclear security summits has really applied a lot of heft and energy to it. There is a political will issue because there are a lot of states that need to do things that look at it and say, I mean, they are not going to go off in my territory if somebody gets a hold of it. So what is in it for me?

Senator KING. Didn't the Pakistanis sell nuclear technology? Or somebody? One of their scientists, as I recall.

Dr. PERKOVICH. Yes. Yes. So that is a real problem. He sold them to states, where there is a distinction. So Iran, North Korea, Libya did not know what to do with it. So it just all sat in a box someplace. So terrorist capability to take all of that and integrate it and produce a weapon is a pretty good stretch. But they did not sell fissile material, which again goes to the point of that.

So as problems go, this one is relatively manageable. It is not to say do not lose sleep over it, you know, but it is relatively—and there is detection. A lot of money has been thrown at detection. It was a good business to be in to make detectors. So, you know, a lot of effort has gone into it.

Senator KING. Dr. Tellis, your thoughts? Are you as sanguine as your colleague?

Dr. TELLIS. Well, I think we have been lucky so far that the kind of proliferation that occurred in Pakistan did not occur in terms of sales to a terrorist group. It occurred to states, and thankfully, as George pointed out, the states essentially did not do very much with it.

But to my mind, as one looks at the nuclear future, this is a risk to which we do not have good answers. Because you could imagine a North Korea-like entity down the line actually taking the fatal step of making certain that some of its nuclear capabilities go to pretty bad people. These are non-state actors, could move to non-state actors.

Senator KING. For whom deterrence is not a concern.

Dr. TELLIS. For whom deterrence—and to deter non-state actors who do not have a sort of certifiable address and who can do things under the cover of darkness is really, you know, that is a hard case to deter.

So what is the strategy? I think the strategy first has to be prevention as best one can. Second, you have to invest a lot in strategic intelligence. Because when people sell things, hopefully, they use telephones, they use computers, they use the Internet. These are things that, in principle, can be intercepted. So you need strategic intelligence.

Third, you need to have a government that is agile enough to, either unilaterally or in collaboration with the international community, to come up with political strategies of interdiction. Sometimes those political strategies may require military components.

So we have to work at all levels. This is not a problem susceptible to a single-point solution.

Senator KING. Yes. Thank you.

Thank you, Mr. Chairman.

Senator SESSIONS. Dr. Kroenig, just one of the things that we have talked about—I do not believe it is fair to say we are acting on—is the possibility of configuring our nuclear arsenal with more specialized weapons that might be usable in a circumstance that would be more targeted and less devastating or have other capabilities.

Have you given any thought to the wisdom of the United States proceeding in that fashion?

Dr. KROENIG. Well, this is an area where I am doing some research now, and I think I share your concerns that it does seem like the United States has a gap in its capabilities at present—a very strong conventional force, a very strong strategic nuclear force, assuming we modernize it—but I think a gap in terms of usable nuclear capabilities.

So the scenario I laid out in my testimony was a conflict between the United States and Russia. Russia is planning and exercising to use nuclear weapons on the battlefield. If that were to happen, if there were——

Senator SESSIONS. So they are planning and exercising in their war games the utilization of nuclear weapons?

Dr. KROENIG. That is right. Nearly——

Senator SESSIONS. Which is beyond what we do?

Dr. KROENIG. President Putin himself sometimes directly participates in these things.

So, if this were to happen, I am afraid that the United States does not really have a good response. We could try to fight through it with conventional capabilities. We could escalate to strategic nuclear warheads, but those are very large warheads. It risks the escalation to a strategic nuclear exchange.

It calls to mind something Dr. Henry Kissinger said in the 1950s, that we could be faced with this choice between suicide or surrender. His argument then was that we needed limited options in between. I think we are in a similar situation now, where we need to think about what are the limited nuclear options we might be able to deploy in response to a limited Russian nuclear attack. Of course, with the point of deterring that attack in the first place.

Senator SESSIONS. Dr. Krepinevich, do you want to comment on that?

Dr. KREPINEVICH. Yes, to add to what Dr. Kroenig said, and in a sense to draw on what George Perkovich said, if you look at the what some people are calling the second nuclear age or the second nuclear era, it is the ability to assess the balance, if you will, is much more difficult because, as George said, of the introduction of advanced precision weapons, advanced defenses, cyber, and so on.

Also because you are looking at a different range of contingencies. You know, a lot of times during the Cold War, we would look at Armageddon. You know, a massive Soviet attack on the United States, and if you could not deter it, it would be the end of the world. We are looking at a wide range of contingencies. We are also, I think, looking at a different—needing to, in a sense, to reconstruct the escalation ladder, and I think that is what a number of these questions are getting at.

If somebody is competing with us at a particular level in the conflict in the Ukraine, as Dr. Kroenig said, could we escalate horizontally? Do we have an advantage in doing so? Can we escalate vertically or horizontally to a different geographic area?

Absent knowing that, absent knowing whether you have the ability to escalate and not jump—not need to jump a number of rungs to—I think Dr. Kroenig's point is to using large-yield, large-scale nuclear weapons, you may preclude yourself from having important options.

I think, personally speaking, the fact that we have not matched what some of our competitors are doing in terms of exploring the options for relatively low-yield weapons or weapons with focused effects limits our options, limits the President's options. I am not talking about more nuclear weapons. I am talking about a greater range of nuclear options, if you will.

One thing I would just add, apropos of what was said earlier in terms of, I guess, what Dr. Tellis said, is I think absolutely what he is talking about, and George as well, about having a strong conventional capability so you have options there. I had conversations with Prime Minister Abe's—one of his senior advisers. He got very emotional and said, "If we were ever hit with a nuclear attack by North Korea, do not tell me you are going to use precision weapons against the North." He said, "You better use nuclear weapons."

Okay, if that is the case and if he really means it, I would rather have the President have the option of using weapons that—perhaps if they are nuclear but have, you know, very focused, very limited effects, you know, that were necessary to do the job.

Senator SESSIONS. Dr. Tellis, I see you nodding on that. You got a brief—

Dr. TELLIS. Well, imagine a world where you have an ideal U.S. nuclear deterrent. To my mind that ideal world would be one where every U.S. nuclear weapon essentially has a selectable yield, and that selectable yield can essentially be—

Senator SESSIONS. A selected yield?

Dr. TELLIS. A selectable yield, where you can actually dial the yield. Where that selectable yield can be organized or orchestrated essentially electronically without someone having to actually go to the weapon and jimmy it up.

I think if you could do that, you give the President, even within the constraints of the current delivery architecture, a whole range ofoptions.

Senator SESSIONS. Well, this is kind of important to us, I think, because we are in a stratified, a calcified process here.

So what you are suggesting is it might be better that if we cannot do as you said, altering it in that fashion but actually could create a multiplicity of weapons with different capabilities that would give the President more option, you think we would do well to consider that in our budgetary and defense posture?

Could all of you all give a quick—I see that Dr. Perkovich——

Dr. TELLIS. Yes.

Dr. PERKOVICH. There are going to be big consequences that, of course, you would want to weigh beyond the budget. I mean, because Matt was talking about lack of capability in Europe, but we are spending—you tell me—I think it is $8 billion to $10 billion to modernize the B61. So if that is irrelevant, why are we going to spend $8 billion to $10 billion to modernize the—so you could save money from that and put it into something else.

But to do that kind of development and procurement, beyond the budgetary issues, will have reverberations within NATO. You want to reassure the alliance. You will split NATO in many ways. So most of the Western European states will—in likelihood would protest that. Their parliaments would be mobilized. The Germans would be mobilized. So you would have a political—

Senator SESSIONS. Their theory is it would be more likely to be used, and so you should not have that option?

Dr. PERKOVICH. Exactly. Exactly. So you get a political fissure within NATO. I am not saying not to do it. I am saying you would want to calculate that.

For every Japanese official who is worried—and I have talked with them, too—like Andrew posits about a threat, you have also got a big constituency in Japan that is anti-nuclear, pro-disarmament, and so on. So you would have to deal with the implication of that.

You would have to deal with how the Chinese would react. How this is a new capability, so they are going to have to counter it. So how do they counter it? How does their counter affect what India does? How does that play back into Pakistan? So all of that kind of assessment would have to go into a decision to change course.

Now, you may still want to do it, but it is not risk free is what I would say.

Senator SESSIONS. Well, I thank you. I have heard a little bit of that.

Senator Donnelly?

Senator DONNELLY. Thank you, Mr. Chairman.

Mr. Kroenig, I want to be careful here because I do not want to go into classified areas. But we have low-yield weapons as well, don't we?

Dr. KROENIG. We do, yes. We have the B61 gravity bombs in Europe, as George pointed out. My concern there is that if Russia used a single nuclear weapon, there are some problems with using the B61 to retaliate.

Senator DONNELLY. There are other missiles, too, though, right?

Dr. KROENIG. There are some air-launched cruise missiles that are based in the United States. But given that they are based in the United States, I think that causes some limits in terms of their ability to function as a deterrent and an assurant in Europe.

I should point out that in my testimony, I do not recommend any specific changes, but I think that we should consider these changes. You know, we are essentially in a third phase in our relations with Russia.

Senator DONNELLY. Well, at what point when you look at Putin, what he is doing, is he trying to change the discussion?

They have lost a lot of their territory. They want to be viewed in a different way. When you look at him—and you know, a lot of people could make a lot of money trying to figure this guy out. But when you look at him, do you think he reasonably thinks that he can use manageable nuclear weapons and not wind up in a total conflagration of his country?

Mr. KOENIG. Based on the way they plan and exercise, I think there is a belief that they could get away with a tailored use of nuclear weapons in the event of a major confrontation with NATO.

So, again, it is not a likely scenario, but nuclear deterrence is really about, you know, dealing with these unlikely, but dangerous situations.

Senator DONNELLY. My expectation is that if Mr. Putin thought that, he would be quickly corrected, and that it would cause one of the most dangerous situations ever seen in this world, and I would think that reasonable Russian leadership would remove him if he tried to move forward with that kind of thing.

Mr. KOENIG. We could hope for that. I think it would be better to have the capabilities in place to deter that kind of response in the first place rather than have them tempted to go down that route and get into a larger confrontation.

Senator DONNELLY. So you mentioned suicide. Do you think we are in a suicide or surrender situation in this country?

Dr. KROENIG. I think if Russia uses tactical nuclear weapons, we do not have a very good response, and so—

Senator DONNELLY. With all of the materials we have, with the nuclear submarines we have, with the triad that we have, you really believe that?

Dr. KROENIG. Well, as I pointed out, I think the problem with the triad is these are large-yield weapons, and so I think that would not have the maybe kind of tailored effect that we might want. In addition, it raises the possibility that Russia would then retaliate with its own strategic weapons.

So, again, I think having—I think we have this gap in our capabilities, and closing that gap would provide a better deterrent.

Dr. PERKOVICH. Can you use cyber? I mean, why does it have to be nuclear? We have all sorts of other capabilities.

What is it that you want to take down, and there are all sorts of ways that you could take it down that do not even necessarily have to be a nuclear weapon.

So is there something that from a deterrent point of view—and there may be—requires it to be a mushroom cloud, or is it to actually incapacitate targets?

Dr. KROENIG. Well, I think these are exactly the kind of questions and discussions we should be having, and I have an ongoing study on this, looking at what the best responses might be.

But, you know, our current capabilities were put in place at the end of the Cold War. All of our assumptions about the strategic environment at the end of the Cold War were that nuclear weapons—the threat of nuclear use between major powers was low. The threat of conflict with Russia was remote, I think was the language we often used. Most people agreed that the strategic environment has fundamentally changed in the past year.

So I think we need to think seriously about what that means for our capabilities. It is possible that we will say that everything we had been doing is exactly right and we should continue to do it, even though the strategic environment has fundamentally shifted. My hunch is that, given that the strategic environment has fundamentally shifted, we will have to change the way we do business.

Senator DONNELLY. Let me ask you about follow-up on Senator King's question about providing defensive weapons to Ukraine. What do you think the effect—and this would be for all of you—what do you think the, you know—I would like to get your ideas. What do you think Russia's response to that would be?

Dr. KROENIG. Would you like me to begin?

Senator DONNELLY. Sure.

Dr. KROENIG. Well, I do think that we should provide defensive weapons to the Ukrainians. I think we should give them the ability to defend themselves. It is difficult to know what Russia's response would be exactly, but the purpose would be to raise the cost to Russia.

I think the worst thing for NATO would be if all of Ukraine fell to Russia. I do not think that is likely in the short term. But if all of Ukraine were to fall to Russia, you can just look at the geography. The rest of NATO would be very much in danger.

So I think doing little things to raise the cost to Russia are in the United States' interests.

Senator DONNELLY. I am out of time, but if we could?

Dr. Perkovich?

Dr. PERKOVICH. In principle, nothing would make me feel better than to colossally humiliate and emasculate President Putin. So, like, I think about ways to do it all the time.

My worry is it would have the reverse effect, and this goes to something Senator King said. Given the geography, given the way that he can operate free of a lot of the political, legal, and other constraints that we have, if one does something that provokes him to feel like he is going to feel even taller as he responds to providing defensive arms to Ukraine—so he comes back harder and says, ''We've never been in Ukraine, but now that NATO has come into Ukraine, we can actually put Russian forces into Ukraine,'' then you have lost that round. It is chess.

So then you come back—at some point, we have to confront the possibility of needing to put air power in as a way to deal with it. But then you run into air defenses and losing pilots.

So unless you have got it figured out, how you do all the escalation so that you kick his—at every step of the way, then why gratify him by going another move that allows him to humiliate the

West further, seems to me very counterproductive to an objective, which I would totally, totally share, which would be to humiliate him.

Senator DONNELLY. Thank you, Mr. Chairman.

Senator SESSIONS. Well, let us finish up.

Dr. Tellis, do you want to have a brief comment on that?

Dr. TELLIS. I share Mr. Perkovich's view, which is if there was a cheap and easy way to put Mr. Putin back in a box, I am all for it.

The problem we have is this. Whatever assistance we contemplate giving the Ukrainians, do we really believe that that assistance by itself will raise the costs to Russia sufficiently to cause Mr. Putin to cease and desist? If we believe that to be the case, there is a compelling argument for providing the aid.

If we believe, on the other hand, that this is only going to be a provocation that will cause Putin to double down on what he is already doing, then you do not do this unless you are prepared to take the fatal next step, which is to introduce NATO or other Western forces to protect the Ukrainians, because they are going to be at the business end of a very severe Russian counter response.

So my view is we should aid them, but if we aid them, we should do it with full malice aforethought. We need to know what we are getting into, and we need to be prepared to pay the price of what will be required to actually stop them.

Senator SESSIONS. Thank you.

Dr. Krepinevich, I think you also wanted to comment on a previous point.

Dr. KREPINEVICH. I think a key issue with respect to Ukraine is just—and I think Ashley was kind of alluding to this—how serious are the Ukrainians?

If they are serious as a heart attack, we have seen recently what even modest amounts of decent military equipment can do to an invading force attempting to occupy another country, whether Iraq or Afghanistan or the Israelis moving into Lebanon in 2006 in the Second Lebanon War. So if they are serious, we have the kinds of equipment that can be very useful for resistance forces, that can buy us a lot of time to get our house in better order and among our Eastern European NATO allies, that can impose dramatically disproportionate costs on the Russians.

So, again, it depends in my mind on just how serious the Ukrainians are. But we can equip them. We do not have to—you know, we can train them outside of Ukraine. There are a number of things we can do and, quite frankly, we have done it before with some success. But I do think, as Ashley said, it requires some serious thinking up front.

As far as the issue of whether new or different kinds of nuclear weapons would help us in the competition with the Russians, I guess my feeling is, bottom line, do you want to buy yourself some more options or don't you? You know, can you make the case—as George was pointing out, you create a bit of dilemma. Can you make the case to your allies that by buying more options, that increases the odds we will not have to use these weapons? Or that we will be put in a position, as Matt was saying, of either go places you do not want to go or surrender, to paraphrase Henry Kissinger.

The other point I would make is there have been a lot of advances in both the social and the cognitive sciences over the last 20–25 years. Two individuals, Kahneman and another, won a Nobel Prize in 2002 for pointing out the fact that there is no such thing as "rational economic man," that human beings are in many ways irrational.

There has also been done—accomplished recently in the social sciences—some work looking across cultures at how people from different cultures calculate cost, benefit, and risk. Obviously, each person within a culture is an individual, but by and large how different cultures tend to view things. In some respects, they can be very different from the way we view things.

So the notion that somehow strategies of deterrence and signaling and so on are going to prove effective over time, certainly Chamberlain thought he was signaling Hitler, I am sure, and thought he had the measure of him. Franklin Roosevelt thought he understood Stalin. We still do not understand why Saddam did the things he did. We think some of them are wholly irrational, I would think.

So to sit here and say that somehow Putin thinks like us, and of course, he would never do these things. History is replete with despots and dictators doing things we never thought they would do, and yes, Khrushchev was removed by his Soviet colleagues in 1964. Unfortunately, 2 years earlier, he precipitated the Cuban Missile Crisis that almost blew the world up.

Senator SESSIONS. Well, thank you.

Now, I will go to you next. You can have my time next.

I would just think that that is wise advice. We had a hundred years ago a shooting of an archduke, and we ended up with the most incredible war that anybody had ever imagined at the time.

On the arming in Ukraine, it is interesting. Brzezinski, Albright, Flournoy have all testified in recent weeks before our committee that we should—Democrats. Secretary Kissinger is cautious. The Germans, Dr. Perkovich, share your view entirely because I was at their embassy not long ago, and they were asked and the ambassador explained their position. So it is a complex world we are in.

Senator King, do you want to—

Senator KING. Well, Dr. Krepinevich, I would like to follow up on your comment.

I think often the fault of American foreign policy is thinking that other people think like us and not understanding what cultural and historic differences, and that is why I am so cautious about Putin. There is, I don't know, 500, 600 years of Russian paranoia going back to Peter the Great about the West. Putin's approval rating in Russia today is 80 percent.

I would venture to say if we came into the Ukraine in a visible way, it would go to 90 percent because it is a nationalistic thing that is just part of our history. I share the chairman's concern about mistakes and accidents.

We heard in our caucus lunch yesterday about Pleiku, a little town in Vietnam, where there was an attack in 1965. Six Americans were killed. As a result of that attack, President Johnson believed that this was directed from North Vietnam, and it justified the bombing campaign and then the introduction of American troops.

It turned out 40 years later, it was a randomly generated local conflict. The whole premise of the escalation was incorrect. That is what really concerns me about the Ukraine, particularly when you are dealing with a place where they have the upper hand in terms of the assets available and readiness—readily available.

I think I want to, though, just come to some consensus. Is it fair to say that all of you agree that we must modernize our nuclear capacity, and second, we must look to greater flexibility in terms of the nuclear deterrent? Is that a fair summary?

Dr. PERKOVICH. Modernization, yes. Flexibility, would depend profoundly on how—and these other effects that I am talking about, because—but modernization, yes.

Senator KING. Dr. Kroenig, that is certainly your position, is it not?

Dr. KROENIG. Yes. Modernization and flexibility.

Senator KING. Thank you.

Dr. KREPINEVICH. Yes.

Senator KING. Thank you.

Thank you, Mr. Chairman.

Senator SESSIONS. Thank you.

Well, just to proceed a little further, Dr. Kroenig and Dr. Tellis.

Dr. Tellis hypothesized—raises the hypothetical that there is an attack on Japan, and we are obligated to respond forcefully on North Korea. If we have a less devastating, more technical weapon, we can honor our requirements, maybe do the necessary job without doing as much destruction as a strategic nuclear weapon might do.

Dr. Kroenig came up with another one I had not thought about, which is what if the Russians use a tactical nuclear weapon in the Ukraine, and do we have a tactical nuclear weapon response, short of a massive strategic response?

I had not thought of either one of those examples before, but I think it is something for us to think about.

As I understand where we are today, the administration favors modernization, but it takes Dr. Perkovich's view that specialization or new weapons, even if they are less dangerous and safer and all that, represent some sort of alteration of our strategy that would cause dominoes around the world to be moved. But I am not sure I agree with that, but that is where we are.

So the budget that has come over, and we have not energized any plan to challenge the President or push him harder, but maybe we should in the months to come and really insist that we discuss this, and is it smarter to have more options or not have more options? So that is—

Dr. Tellis?

Dr. TELLIS. I would just like to respond to that because I accept the basic argument that Senator Donnelly is making, that the U.S. arsenal certainly has weapons of varying yield, including low yields.

What I do not have an answer to, at unclassified levels certainly that I can think of, is whether these weapons meet the tests of responsiveness and penetrability. I think that is really what you need to think about in a different forum. If you conclude that the low-yield weapons or the weapons that have selectable yields meet the requirements of responsiveness and penetrability, then I think we are home free, and we do not have to worry about this.

But in general, I think the point that Dr. Krepinevich made is really the central point, which is, do you want to be in a position where you have more options rather than less, particularly as you enter a nuclear world where most of the emerging nuclear powers are going to have weapons that are relatively small in yield and, you know, in small numbers?

So as you think of this new world that is emerging out there, the questions that Dr. Kroenig is asking is whether the legacy force can actually deal with these contingencies without modification. Now I do not know whether this requires us to actually go back and develop new warheads or whether we can simply tinker with what we have in the back rooms. But these are questions that I think need to be addressed in classified settings with folks in STRATCOM [U.S. Strategic Command].

Senator DONNELLY. Yes, there are a lot of classified settings to address these in. I guess, you know, we talk about people, in effect, almost riding by each other without understanding that they just stopped on the same street.

I would think, and maybe it is for publication, if President Putin would ever think that he could use a low-yield nuclear weapon on another country without catastrophic events then beginning from that, I think he would be sadly mistaken, that every other leader in our network of friends would take action.

I think—I would hope, you know, as you talk about this, it is a different culture. It is a different way of thinking. It is in many ways sometimes ships passing in the night, but one ship needs to tell the other ship, "If you do this, all bets are off."

Dr. Perkovich?

Dr. PERKOVICH. Just to reinforce—and I agree with Ashley, you would want to do these studies. You would also want to ask all the different commands, like, given $10 billion for this or for that, how would you spend the money?

But beyond that, in my travels—and I have been to all the countries that we are talking about—Iran, not North Korea, but all of the targets. I do not think their leaders are going to discriminate between whether it was 100 kilotons or 12 kilotons, and so on. I do not think if a device goes off, you know, over at the Pentagon and we are sitting here, somebody is going to say, "Don't worry, it was only 30 kilotons, you know, it wasn't a big one."

So I think it is a game theoretic calculation in a lot of ways, and that this is something the Chinese and others understood all along. They have got their 250 weapons, we have got our 2,200—that you do not need to have—that they are political weapons, and the distinctions about yields and all of that are something that people like us get paid to think about, but political decision-makers in an actual event when they are going off probably are not going to be making those distinctions in the way that they then react. So I would factor that into the discussion, too.

Senator SESSIONS. Now, Dr. Krepinevich, what about the triad? Some think we could get by without the full triad. Maybe the nuclear subs and/or something in addition.

Do you four have an opinion as to that? It is not as expensive as you—as some people imagine, but it is an expensive proposition.

What are your thoughts about the triad?

Dr. KREPINEVICH. My thought is that until we identify a range of contingencies, realistic contingencies that reflect the circumstances that myself and my colleagues have been describing here, and test the arsenal against those contingencies or scenarios, I would be loathe to abandon any of the legs of the triad.

I think the bomber leg gives us an enormous amount of flexibility. The submarine leg certainly, perhaps, allows us to sleep most securely at night. The land-based missile force, to a certain extent, acts as kind of a missile sump because if you look historically at the studies of nuclear attack and so on, that it gives us the ability to absorb a lot of an adversary's nuclear capability if they want to undertake a first strike against us.

So, again, I think we are putting the cart before the horse if we are talking about abandoning a particular leg of the triad without looking at the new circumstances in which we find ourselves, and how we would deal with those circumstances across a range of plausible contingencies.

Senator SESSIONS. Thank you, and I will go to you, but do any of the other three want to share briefly?

Senator DONNELLY. I apologize. I have to go to another meeting right now.

But I want to thank all of you. We are in your debt for your service, for your efforts to inform us in the best possible decisions we can make. I want to thank you so much for taking the time to be here.

Thank you.

Senator SESSIONS. Dr. Kroenig?

Dr. KROENIG. Yes, on the triad, I would agree that each leg of the triad has special attributes and characteristics and that our nuclear force would be weaker if we got rid of any of the legs. I do think we need all three.

You mentioned the cost issue as well, and I think according to most estimates, we spend something like 4 percent of the defense budget on the strategic forces. Given, as Dr. Tellis said, that it is really the backstop of the rest of our defensive capabilities, I think that is well worth it.

Even Secretary of Defense Carter has been on the record to say that I think the quote is, ''Nuclear weapons don't actually cost that much.'' So I think these arguments that they are too expensive miss the mark.

Senator SESSIONS. He shared that with me recently, and I share that view.

Are there any of you like to comment on that?

Dr. PERKOVICH. My only thing would be, I agree with you, one would study it. It would be progress if we could make it, and you could help make it, not a holy trinity. In other words, that it is—the triad is something that should be scrutinized, analyzed, and you come up with strong justification, you keep doing it. But for a long time it has been something you could not question, and I think that would be progress to say we ought to analyze it and not prejudge one way or the other. That would be progress.

Dr. KREPINEVICH. I just would like to say, Mr. Chairman, my colleague Todd Harrison and Evan Montgomery are working on a cost estimate of the nuclear enterprise, and we are looking to release that estimate in April.

Senator SESSIONS. Well, that was going to be my final question to ask all of you, knowing what you know about the budget, the President's budget is public, to give us any thoughts about what the priorities should be and if it is sufficient.

Dr. Tellis, do you want to——

Dr. TELLIS. Senator, I cannot speak to the issues of cost. So I will defer to Dr. Krepinevich on that.

But I wanted to just make the point that when one looks at the nuclear trend lines 10–20 years out, there is nothing that compels me to conclude that you can move away from the triad anytime soon. So I hope that is something that we will continue to invest in.

Senator SESSIONS. Thank you.

I am, frankly, of the view that there is uncertainty about the United States' will around the world. I do not think it is correct, but there is a growing uncertainty out there. I think that any significant reduction in our nuclear capabilities could be misread at this point in history in a way it might not be misread previously, like Nixon going to China kind of insight.

I also have been—Dr. Krepinevich, I have been watching the defense budget, trying to be hard on them, but likewise, I am a little bit of the view that things are getting dicey around the world. People think we are on a pell-mell collapse of will, and even the defense budget, if it is cut—if it is perceived as being reduced too significantly could be improperly perceived as weakness.

Because I think we can maintain a lean-type budget. With this fabulous military, this battle-hardened, fully equipped military that we have, and highly trained, I do not think we are heading pell-mell to weakness. But I am worried we got people in the United States that think so, and we got people around the world that share that concern.

Thank you for this fascinating and fabulous comments you shared with us. Again, if you have any thoughts that you would like to share, I would appreciate receiving them.

I would also say that we have a good subcommittee and a good committee that I do think wants to do the right thing, and politics has not been a big factor in recent years on nuclear issues, and I hope we can keep it that way.

Thank you.

[Whereupon, at 4:25 p.m., the subcommittee adjourned.]

www.ingramcontent.com/pod-product-compliance
Lightning Source LLC
Chambersburg PA
CBHW081852280526
45789CB00007B/2672

* 9 7 8 1 5 4 2 3 1 3 2 6 1 *